Emmanuel, God With Us —

Studies

in

Matthew

Emmanuel, God With Us —
Studies in Matthew

Harold H. Etling

BMH Books
Winona Lake, Indiana 46590

Cover photo: A street scene in
Jerusalem (Photo by H. Armstrong
Roberts).

ISBN: 0-88469-107-1

COPYRIGHT 1979
BMH BOOKS
WINONA LAKE, INDIANA

Printed in U.S.A.

Foreword

Many books have been written with the Gospels as their background. The probable reason is the richness of the soil has attracted so many to search for still more truths. It seems that each who work this soil comes up with still more insight and helps for us. *Emmanuel, God With Us,* written by Dr. Harold Etling, proves this to be a fact that he who opens his mind to the leading of the Lord will come away with more spiritual instructions from God.

This study guide has for its purpose an overview of the Book of Matthew and is intended for the person who wants to understand the whole picture of this first book of the New Testament. The guide is one of a series dealing with the Bible and has its useful purpose in Sunday School series as well as home Bible study.

Dr. Harold Etling is now with the Lord and this manuscript was prepared by him for study in Sunday School classes at the adult level. Dr. Etling was unusually well prepared for this writing. He was a pastor for a number of years. Then for 19 years, he was the leader of the Christian Education Department of the Fellowship of Grace Brethren Churches. He served in Christian education and Sunday School work at the national level throughout the United States. To his many friends who knew and loved him, as well as many who will learn from him for the first time, I know this book will be a blessing and bring you to a greater knowledge and love of the Saviour.

—Charles W. Turner
Executive Editor, BMH Books
March 1979

Table of Contents

Foreword 5

1. The Man and the Book 7

2. Emmanuel—God With Us 17

3. The Childhood of Jesus 27

4. The Preparation and Initiation of Jesus
   into His Ministry 37

5. The Teaching of the King Concerning
   the Kingdom 49

6. The King Reveals His Power 61

7. Expanded Witness—Widening Gulf 71

8. The Mysteries of the Kingdom of Heaven 83

9. Training of the Twelve 95

10. Signposts on the Road 109

11. Jesus' Last Journey to Jerusalem 121

12. Passion Week Activities 133

13. The Suffering, Death and Resurrection of Jesus ... 145

1

An Introduction to the Gospel According to Matthew

~~~~~~

The Man and the Book

THE CHAPTER OUTLINED:

INTRODUCTION
BACKGROUND
   I.   The Persian Empire
  II.   The Grecian Empire
 III.   The Roman Empire
BIBLE STUDY
   I.   Matthew the Man
      (a)   The call of Matthew (Matt. 9:9-17)
      (b)   The commissioning of Matthew (Matt. 10:2-3)
  II.   The Book of Matthew
      (a)   The title
      (b)   The chronology
      (c)   The purpose and message of the book

INTRODUCTION

Although the Book of Matthew appears first in order in our New Testament, there is much evidence that it was not the first of the New Testament books written. It is probable that several of Paul's Epistles precede the date of Matthew as to time of writing. However, the chronological story of the birth of Jesus ought to come first and this is found in Matthew.

Text: Matthew 9:9-13; 10:2-3.

BACKGROUND

From the Book of Malachi to the Book of Matthew there is a period of history which involves about 400 years of time in which God remained silent. Apparently no word came from heaven to earth. No prophet spoke; no book was written which claimed God as its author! It is a period often called the 400 years of silence. At the close of the Old Testament the Jews were a part of the Persian Empire. The Jews were looking for the fulfillment of the prophecies concerning their coming Messiah, and the New Testament opens with this statement: "The book of the generation of Jesus Christ, the son of David, the son of Abraham." Thus our Lord is instantly identified as the Messiah, the antitype of Old Testament history, the fulfillment of the Davidic Covenant (cf. II Sam. 7:8-16), and the climax of the Abrahamic Covenant of Promise (Gen. 12:3).

I. The Persian Empire

In the closing days of the Old Testament we see the transfer of political power. The end comes to the Babylonian rule, and the beginnings of the Persian reign are recorded in the pages of the Old Testament. Cyrus, king of Persia (cf. Ezra 1:1), had conquered the Medes, and as they joined forces with him, they had together conquered Babylon in 539 B.C. The decree of Cyrus in 537 B.C. brought about the return of the first party of exiles, led by Zerubbabel and the priest Jeshua. Ezra and Nehemiah followed much later; Ezra in

458 B.C. and Nehemiah in 445 B.C. The beginning of the period between Malachi and Matthew is concerned with the closing years of the Persian Empire, from 433 to 333 B.C. During this period, in spite of wars both to the east and west, the land of Palestine remained practically undisturbed. The people of Israel who came back from the exile in Babylon came back cured of the sin of idolatry. With the abolishment of idolatry, and nonconformity to the nations around them, there arose an utter contempt among the Jews for the surrounding nations. The system called "Seribism" emphasized the separateness of Jewish blood and exalted Israel's one remaining glory, the "law." When Ezra returned to Jerusalem (cf. Ezra 7:11), he became the first of a group of scribes who devoted themselves to the preservation, study and exposition of the law, carefully regarding the letter of it, but disregarding the spirit (cf. Luke 11:42-44; II Cor. 3:6). This background began to sow the seeds of the worst features of Pharisaism.

During their stay in Babylon, away from the Temple and its services, the Jews developed a simple form of worship, with its stress upon the reading of the law, which came to be associated with the synagogue. An outgrowth of the meetings held in the synagogues for the teaching of the law was the addition of prayers and preaching. The meetings which were held on Sabbath days, and feast days, came also to be associated with the synagogue. An outgrowth of the meetings held in the synagogues for the teaching of the law was the addition of prayers and preaching. The meetings which were held on Sabbath days, and feast days, came also to be held on other days, and at the same hours with the services in the Temple. Parenthetically, it might be added that the Christian church owes much to the synagogue so far as worship and order are concerned.

Then too, during this period the position of the high priest came to new prominence. The Persian governor lived in a palace overlooking the Temple area, but the Persians were quite content to leave the rule of the Jews largely in the hands of the high priest. He became the key leader of the Jews, but a political instrument in the hands of the Persians.

One other important outgrowth of this period was the Sanhedrin. Most students believe that it originated as an advisory council in the days of Ezra, the scribe, but became increasingly important through the years.

The exiles brought back with them the Aramaic language; and while Hebrew remained the language of the Temple, Aramaic became the language of the people. Jesus Himself spoke some in Aramaic (cf. Mark 5:41; 15:34).

II. The Grecian Empire

The Persians had never been able to extend westward into Europe. The Grecians had resisted again and again. By the year 336 B.C. under the leadership of Alexander, Greece was ready for world conquest. By 330 B.C. the Persian Empire was completely under Alexander's control.

Alexander was friendly to the Jews, and after the city of Alexandria had been founded in Egypt the Jews were welcomed. Soon there were more Jews in Egypt than in Palestine itself. With the development of commerce between Africa, Europe and Asia, as a result of Alexander's triumphs; the Jews were scattered abroad, making ready the strategic beachheads for the coming of Christian missionaries (cf. Acts 15:21).

Alexander died in 323 B.C., and soon his empire was torn apart by the quarrel of his successors, so that by 315 B.C. four kingdoms had emerged—Macedonia, Thrace, Syria with Mesopotamia, and Egypt with southern Syria (cf. Dan. 8:21-22). For more than 100 years Palestine was ruled from the south by the dynasty of the Ptolemies in Egypt, a rule which continued with the exception of two short intervals until 198 B.C. when Antiochus III, a powerful king of Syria, gained control of the land from the north. It was during this century of rule of the Ptolemies (Ptolemy Philadelphus the ruler from 285-247 B.C.) that the translation of a Greek version of the Old Testament was encouraged. The volume produced by 70 Jewish scholars was named after these scholars, and the Septuagint continued to be of vital importance during the early days of the New Testament.

Grecian influence made marked imprint upon the life of the Jewish leadership and customs, which eventually served to divide Jewish leadership into two parties, the Hellenizers, who favored Grecian ideas and ways, and the Separatists, who clung to the traditions of their fathers and believed firmly in the separations that Ezra had preached.

In 198 B.C. Palestine passed under the control of the Syrian or Selucid kings. In 176 B.C. Antiochus Epiphanes, "a king of fierce countenance," came to the throne. He was an aggressive Hellenizer and was determined to draw his subjects together by imposing and enforcing Greek ways upon them. In 167 B.C. he determined to stamp out Judaism forever, and quickly wrecked the Temple, erected a status of the Olympian Zeus within the Temple court, and offered a sow upon the altar of burnt offering (cf. Dan. 11:31).

The first serious resistance was offered by an aged priest, Mattathias, who slew a Syrian officer who had come to enforce the decrees of Antiochus. This was the signal for revolt, and after the priest died, leadership fell into the hands of Judas Maccabaeus. Under his leadership, the Syrians were driven back on the 25th of the Jewish month Chisleu, in 165 B.C., the Temple was cleansed, and daily sacrifices were restored in Jerusalem. This great event was celebrated as the Feast of Dedication, of which reference is made in John 10:22.

The history during the next century was that of a civil war as we see two distinct parties of the Jews emerging. Those who favored Grecian tendencies, tracing themselves to Zadok, the priest, became known as Sadducees, the sons of Zadok. The Separatists drew into still greater exclusiveness and determined to make a hedge around the law, thus becoming known as the separate ones—Pharisees. Constant strife between these two parties continued; and for the first time, we hear in Jewish history of death by crucifixion when 200 Pharisees were put to death on the cross.

III. The Roman Empire

In the midst of this constant strife and the battle of the two brothers for power, the sons of Alexander Jannaeus and Alexandria, the Romans appear on the scene. In the year 63 B.C. after a siege of 3 months, and the massacre of 12,000 Jews, Jerusalem was crushed and Pompey entered the holy of holies in the Temple. He was amazed to find no idol or object of worship. The holy of holies bore testimony of the fact of true spiritual worship as God originally intended for His people. Now, Galilee and Samaria were divided into two separate districts, and Jewish independence had come to an end. Finally, in 37 B.C. the Romans decreed that Herod should be the king of the Jews. He returned to the city, and became a "hated" ruler of the Jews. He rebuilt the temple on a scale that eclipsed the original. The existence of a Herodian party in New Testament times indicates that some accepted him (Mark 3:6; 12:13). He was a fearful king on the throne; who, when apprised of the coming of the Lord Jesus as King of the Jews, caused the massacre of the innocents.

From Malachi to Matthew, we have now arrived at the days of Herod the King (Matt. 2:1).

BIBLE STUDY

I. Matthew the Man

(a) **The call of Matthew (Matt. 9:9-17).** The calling of this tax gatherer has often been called "a miracle of grace," and some have said that the reason for including it at the particular place in the book indicates that none of the other miracles described in the chapter was so great a wonder, or required such an exhibition of power and grace, as the conversion of Matthew. This call is included with several miracles which Jesus performed and recorded in chapters 8 and 9.

It is evident that these did not all take place in the exact order of time, but rather, are massed together, so as to produce a strong impression. Jesus had just taught the disciples the great truths of the Sermon on the Mount, so now He demonstrates His authority as a teacher. These were proofs that God the Father was with Him and had sent Him. He illustrated His teaching by giving object lessons through the miracles He performed.

"And as Jesus passed forth" (9:9), apparently from His house in Capernaum where He had healed a paralytic (vv. 1-8). Mark helps us just a bit at this point by suggesting that Jesus went out again by the seaside (Mark 2:13). Here He "saw a man named Matthew." Both Mark and Luke tell us it was Levi who was sitting at the receipt of custom. Levi, his name as a publican—tax gatherer, was now to be called Matthew. Publicans in Palestine were tax collectors for the Roman emperor. The work of collecting revenue in various cities was distributed generally by the governor of the province, who set a certain annual sum to be delivered to him by the publican occupying an office, and anything collected beyond that, the publican could keep. We have a name for it in our own generation—"political graft," or in the past it has been called "a squeeze." The Jews hated these publicans, even as some citizens of our own nation hate the tax collector, although not with the same kind of hatred. In that day, they were forced, for the sake of the publican, to pay exorbitant taxes; and hence, the Jews classed publicans, harlots and sinners all together. A publican was not only guilty of theft, but the Jews looked upon him as a traitor to Israel. He was not permitted to worship in the synagogue, his own family was socially ostracized, and he had no fellowship with the decent citizens of his community. The Talmud actually regards a publican's repentance as impossible. No money known to have come from them was received for religious uses.

Now Jesus comes to Levi, and our text reminds us that He simply said, "Follow me." Dr. Wilbur Smith suggests that he has always felt that there are at least four great truths in this call to Matthew. First of all, Jesus held out hope for one whom everyone else despised. Second, He wanted this man to be with Him or He would not have said, "Follow me." Third, He told Matthew what to do, and whatever Jesus tells anyone to do is right. When we disobey His command we are impoverishing ourselves. Finally, in following Christ, Matthew would have to leave the nefarious business in which he was engaged. One cannot walk in opposite directions at the same time, and to follow Jesus is to walk away from sin. Matthew had lived a life of monetary affluence, but one of social and spiritual ostracism. Now he is invited to follow, and ultimately to use the pen with which he had falsified the accounts of his countrymen to write this book.

(b) The commissioning of Matthew (Matt. 10:2-3). One other thing we discover about the man who wrote the book, namely, his commissioning. For a number of months, Jesus had been taking these men with Him wherever He went. He had been training them in the work by taking them with Him, and the evidence is that they had been on at least two tours through Galilee. He did not expect them to do their work without some previous preparation. He invited them to follow Him; then He took them with Him wherever He went. Finally, He endued them with power and authority to do the work; that is, He both qualified them and authorized them.

Several practical thoughts are evident here:

1. Perhaps one reason why Jesus chose a publican for such high office was to leave an object lesson of hope for all— even the most disreputable of men. None are too far away from God but that they can be brought into perfect fellowship with Him.

2. Another reason for choosing a publican might be found in the fact that in Christ we are made one; for in Him there is neither Jew nor Gentile, rich nor poor, bond nor free. All men are on an equal footing when they come to the cross.

3. The fact that the story of the banquet in Matthew's

house follows his call, indicates another possible reason for his calling and commissioning. As a publican, he could reach men that others might not reach.

4. This call shows how God can take the talents of a business man, and use them in His work, even as He did Matthew's pen, to write a story of the Gospel.

II. The Book of Matthew

(a) **The title.** The book is generally referred to as "The Gospel of Matthew," but in reality, it would be better titled, "The Gospel According to Matthew." There is but one Gospel, although in the first four books of the New Testament, we have four complementary accounts.

(b) **The chronology.** It is generally agreed that this book was written shortly before the destruction of Jerusalem in A.D. 70. References to the "temple" (24:1-2), the "holy place" (v. 15), impending trouble (vv. 16-20) and to the "holy city" (27:53) indicate Jerusalem had not yet fallen. The expression "unto [or until] this day" (27:8, 28:15) indicates a period of years from the events referred to, but 20 years would satisfy these passages.

Matthew wrote shortly before Luke and almost certainly Luke wrote in the years A.D. 58-60. This would place Matthew's writing at about A.D. 58. The evidence points to the writing of the book in Palestine, perhaps in Jerusalem itself.

The book covers in chronology the life of Christ, from birth to death, followed by a few post-resurrection stories.

(c) **The purpose and message of the book.** Matthew has a special object in his account of the Gospel; namely, to show the Jews that Jesus is the long-expected Messiah, the Son of David, and that His life fulfilled the Old Testament prophecies. This purpose is at least alluded to as he begins the book, "The book of the generation of Jesus Christ, the son of David, the son of Abraham" (Matt. 1:1). This statement links Christ with two of the great covenants that God made: one with David, which was the promise of a king to sit upon his throne forever (II Sam. 7:8-13); the other with Abraham which promised that through him all the families of the earth should be blessed (Gen. 12:3).

David's son was a king. Abraham's son was a sacrifice. Matthew opens with the birth of a king and closes with the offering of a sacrifice. The purpose of Matthew then reaches from the royal genealogy given in the first chapter to the inscription on the cross: "THIS IS JESUS THE KING OF THE JEWS" (Matt. 27:37). To further show that this is the Book of the King, we note that the word "kingdom" is used 55 times; "kingdom of heaven"—32 times; "Son of David"—7 times.

Matthew has pictured Jesus as the Messiah King and thus the message is based upon this picture. It is the story of the King. The Sermon on the Mount is a manifesto of the King and this is followed in chapters 8 and 9 by a manifestation of the powers of Christ to cure all the diseases that afflict humanity.

The entire book is a record of the providential care of God for His own, in spite of the attacks of Satan working through every means, including wicked men, to destroy the work of God.

Jesus Christ, the Son of God and the Son of Man, is providentially cared for in the midst of fierce hatred and antagonism until He has accomplished His work.

Hallelujah! What a Saviour—What a King!

2

Matthew 1:1-25

▬▬▬▬▬▬▬▬▬▬▬▬▬▬▬▬▬▬▬▬

Emmanuel – God With Us

THE CHAPTER OUTLINED:

INTRODUCTION
THE EXPOSITION
   I.   The Genealogies of the Messiah (Matt. 1:1-17)
  II.   The Conception of the Messiah (Matt. 1:18)
 III.   The Annunciation to Joseph (Matt. 1:19-21)
 IV.   The Confirmation of the Record by Matthew
       (Matt. 1:22-25)
       (a)   A fulfillment of prophecy (v. 23)
       (b)   The obedience of Joseph (vv. 24-25)

INTRODUCTION

The Old Testament is literally filled with prophecies of Messiah's coming to the earth; now the writers of the Gospel record it as an event that has become a matter of history. Beginning with the first promise of "the seed of the woman" as found in Genesis 3:15, the prophecies become more numerous as we follow promises of God through the Old Testament. In Micah 5:2 the very place of His birth is announced many years prior to His coming to the earth. Micah was a contemporary of Isaiah in the period of 750-710 B.C., and so specific is his prophecy concerning the birthplace of the Lord, that it defies fulfillment except by the miraculous hand of God, the Creator, who now appears in the person of Jesus, "Emmanuel . . . God with us."

Isaiah, who prophesied in the same period, 700 years prior to the coming of Jesus to the earth, gave us the prophecy which Matthew tells us is now fulfilled.

THE EXPOSITION

In the Greek language the words with which Matthew begins this book prove exceedingly interesting. They are "biblos geneseos" meaning, "the book of the generation," or "the book of the beginning." Our word "bibliography" comes from "biblos," as also ultimately the word "Bible." Our word "genesis" of course, comes directly from the second word. It is extremely interesting that each one of the four recorders of the story of Christ begins with some reference to "the beginning" of something related to Christ. In the first verse of Matthew, we have the word "genesis" or "generation." In Mark's record it is—"The beginning of the gospel of Jesus Christ." Luke, in his prologue, speaks of those who "from the beginning were eyewitnesses." John begins His record in a different manner: "In the beginning was the Word."

I. The Genealogies of the Messiah (Matt. 1:1-17)

This is one of the two genealogies of Christ found in the New Testament—this one beginning with Abraham and end-ing with Joseph, while the other found in Luke 3:23-28 begins with Jesus and goes back to Adam. The Greeks, for whom Luke wrote, were interested in mankind in general; but the Jews, for whom Matthew wrote, were more interested in a record that traced the family back to their father Abraham. Time of presentation would forbid the study of each one mentioned in the ancestry. However, some general observations are worthwhile. (a) Matthew gives us 3 sets of 14 generations each. This was perhaps done to assist the reader in remembrance. Really, the sense of "begat" does not of necessity mean all that has been read into it. Actually, the word indicates either immediate or remote descent, and may refer either to father or grandfather. The time from Abraham to David was 840 years; from David to captivity, 460; from the captivity to Christ, 590 years. (b) The repetition of reference to David is of real importance. Five times in three verses, David is mentioned (vv. 1, 6, 17). There can be little doubt that Matthew is interested in giving proof to the world of the Davidic background of Jesus. The emphasis on Christ's Davidic descent entitling Him to the Throne in Israel often appears in the New Testament, for example: Matthew 21:9; Acts 2:29-30; 13:22-23; Romans 1:3; II Timothy 2:8; Revelation 5:5, 22:16. (c) Contrary to Hebrew practice, Matthew names five women in the genealogy; four of these have a shadow over them. Thamer [Tamar] (v. 3) conceived by her father-in-law, Judah (Gen. 38); Rahab was a harlot (Joshua 2); Ruth was a Moabitess, a descendant of Lot by his own daughter (Gen. 19:36-37), and the law stated that no Moabite was to enter into the congregation (Deut. 23:3-4); Bathsheba was the wife of Uriah, with whom David sinned (II Sam. 11). Dr. Wilbur Smith remarked on the inclusion of women in the genealogy: "The inclusion of these women shows on the one hand, that Christ's sinlessness was not due to a sinless ancestry, and, on the other hand, it was a revelation of God's purpose to redeem sinners."

To have a genealogy that continued in the manner in which

the ancestry of Christ continued is in itself a miracle; for it was necessary for God to carefully guard this family tree for more than 2,000 years. (d) It is likewise very significant that with the genealogy of Christ, genealogies in the Word of God cease. We have none for John the Apostle nor for Paul. In reality, we do not know the names of most of the parents of the apostles. With the coming of Christ, and his subsequent death and resurrection, there has come a new thing into the world. Christ becomes the head of the new race, of those who receive Him as their Saviour. He is the second Adam, for those who become the sons of God by the new birth.

II. The Conception of the Messiah (Matt. 1:18)

There is a long, beautiful, minute account of the miraculous conception of Jesus recorded in Luke 1:26-38. Matthew does not give so much detail, and yet sums up the story in this one verse. We need to see (a) the Person that was born into the world, "Jesus Christ." He was different from any other person ever born into the world. When you and I came into the world, we were new persons, never having existed before. When the Lord Jesus came into this world, He was not a new person. He was the eternal Son of God, who now took upon himself the form of a man. He was born of a woman, and by His own choice now actually lives as a member of the human race upon the earth. Prior to this time, He had been with the Father in glory. If He had come into the world by natural union of a husband and wife, He would have been a monstrosity, for He was the preexistent Son of God. For this second person of the Godhead to be conceived in the womb of the Virgin Mary, and be born of her, of necessity required divine intervention. This is exactly what we have in the story of the birth of Christ recorded by both Matthew and Luke. The virgin birth is in conformity with all that we know of His subsequent life. Even the critics of the virgin birth will admit that both historically and logically, the divinity of Christ and the incarnation are bound up with the virgin birth. We cannot maintain one without the other.

There is one other item that is tied closely with the virgin birth. The entire story of the life of Christ from birth to death sets forth His absolute sinlessness. He could not have been our sacrifice if He had any taint of sin in His life. Here is a moral phenomenon which cannot be explained by natural law. This one Person, is the only person who ever lived upon the earth in 6,000 years of human history, who has lived every minute of His life pleasing God in every detail of thought, word and deed. He was without sin! The miracle of a sinless life demands among other things a miraculous entrance into the world of man. Of course, there are questions that arise. Does not the fact of His coming into the world, even though He came by miraculous conception, involve His acquiring of a sinful nature from His mother? Mary was a member of the human race and had a sinful nature even as we have sinful natures. Why, then, was the sinful nature of Mary not passed along to her son? The answer must be in the fact that not only was Jesus divinely conceived by the Holy Spirit, but Mary, during all the months that intervened between His conception and His birth, was overshadowed by the same Holy Spirit (cf. Luke 1:35). The longer we study the story of the conception and birth of the Lord Jesus, the more we are convinced that we must conclude that it would have been unnatural if the birth of our Saviour had been natural. It is a miracle!

III. The Annunciation to Joseph (Matt. 1:19-21)

We discover a little bit of background here, concerning Joseph, the husband-to-be of Mary. The previous record (v. 18) told us that before the marriage was consummated, Mary was "found with child of the Holy Ghost," but this had not been made known to Joseph. Now, he is described as "a just man" (v. 19), a strict observer of the law. We must remember that the law for unfaithfulness was very strict (Deut. 22:23-24), but its severity had been somewhat lessened through a process of divorce. Divorce could be effected publicly, so that the shame of the woman might be seen by all; or it could be done privately, by the method of giving the bill of separation to the woman in the presence of two witnesses. Joseph was not willing to make Mary a public example, but "was minded to put her away privily [privately]." However, before that event took place, an angel appeared to him in a dream, telling him not to be afraid to marry Mary, since the conception was of the Holy Ghost; and beyond this, her child would be a son, and Joseph was to name Him, "Jesus." The angel knew two things before the Lord came into the world: (a) The babe to be born was to be a son. A question always in the hearts and minds of expectant parents is whether the babe will be a boy or a girl. Not so with Mary, or with Joseph, the man engaged to Mary. The angel said Mary would bring forth "a son." (b) The angel also revealed the life purpose of this son: His name was to be called Jesus, "for he shall save his people from their sins." In the natural world, not only must we await the birth, but actually the fulfillment of growth, until the babe that is born has grown into manhood or womanhood, before we discover even the place of his or her labors. Although many mothers would hope that their son would become a great leader of people, or their daughter would become a real example among women, none of us can predict the outcome. The angel knew, and therefore was able to speak clearly, "he shall save his people from their sins."

The name "Jesus" is the most beautiful name, the best-known name in all the world. It has become the theme of more songs than any other one word in the human language. Think of all the songs you know that are written about Jesus. Yet, how little of this message from the angel is known by the world. The name "Jesus" is the Greek form of the Hebrew word "Joshua" which is an abbreviation of the name "Jehoushua" from two words, "Jah" and "Yasha" meaning "to save." This word occurs for the first time in the Bible in Exodus 14:30 in the story in which God is saving Israel from her enemies. The name "Jesus" occurs more than 600 times in this record of Matthew, and more than 500 times in the 4 gospel records.

The name "Jesus" given to Christ first by the angel, meaning "Jehovah saves" is a revelation of the purpose for which Christ came into the world—to save His people from their sins, and with it all of the power of sin, including hell and death, and fear of every kind. When John the Baptist first introduced Him, he simply said: "Behold, the Lamb of God, which taketh away the sin of the world" (John 1:29). In this hour when men are using the name in so many ways, we need to remember that there was but one purpose for the coming of Jesus into the world; for He came to die for the sins of the world, and that means He died for us.

IV. The Confirmation of the Record by Matthew (Matt. 1:22-25)

The story of the annunciation and subsequent birth of Christ was given to Matthew by the Holy Spirit. Now, there is further confirmation in a written conclusion to the matter of Christ's birth.

(a) **A fulfillment of prophecy (v. 23).** First of all, Matthew tells us clearly that the coming of Christ into the world by this supernatural conception is the fulfillment of the prophecy written hundreds of years before. "Emmanuel" in verse 23 is only used in the New Testament in relation to the birth of Christ and means "God with us." This word occurs twice in Isaiah (Isa. 7:14; 8:8) and is not used again until in our Scripture passage. This means that although there is as much difference between God and man as there can possibly be between the infinite and the finite, now the infinite God has taken upon himself the form of a man—the infinite God now dressed in human form has taken upon himself the form of the finite being which He created. He did this in order to show His own love, which involves His own sacrifice, in order to reveal His redeeming love. The late J. D. Jones in preaching on this text says of Christ's becoming one of us: "I should argue for the naturalness and almost inevitability of the incarnation on two grounds. I should argue it, first, from the nature of God himself. If God is a personal being, it is natural that He should reveal himself . . . I do not and cannot believe in a deaf and dumb God. I believe in a God who can and who will hold intercourse with the creatures He made. And I should argue it, in the second place, from the nature of man. The characteristic of man is this, he is *capax Dei*— that is, he has a capacity for God. He is a moral and spiritual being. This at once makes incarnation possible and likely."

(b) **The obedience of Joseph (vv. 24-25).** In verse 19, we read that Joseph was "a just man"; and now here, we discover that he was likewise "an obedient man." He manifested obedience to the message he had received from God. He had intended when he went to bed, to put Mary, his espoused wife away. During the nighttime the angel of God came to direct him in another manner. Now, we read that Joseph "being raised from sleep did as the angel of the Lord had bidden him, and took unto him his wife." Have you ever thought of what might have been the outcome, if Joseph had acted on his first impulse, and put Mary away immediately when it was told him that she was with child? He took time to wait upon God; and God, without doubt in answer to Joseph's inquiry to Him, sent the messenger with the directions. Here is a very practical lesson for all of us. If there are problems, we ought to search out the Word of God and wait for the direction of God for the best results. Now, Joseph moves to put into action the directions God sent. It involved three things: (a) he took unto him his wife; knowing the possibility of questions and criticisms of his friends and family; (b) he "knew her not till she had brought forth her first-born son." The physical union was not completed until after the babe was born. There are those who teach that physical union was never consummated, thus denying that there were other children born into this household. The very language used here, however, does not indicate this. He "knew her not till she had brought forth her firstborn son" seems to be very clear evidence that after the birth of Jesus, Joseph and Mary did consummate the physical union and gave to the world natural children, some of whom became disciples of this supernatural Son, "God with us." (c) "He called his name JESUS," the sweetest name on earth. This is the climax of the story from the pen of Matthew. Joseph was obedient to the smallest detail, even the naming of the babe, thus giving to the world understanding of just who this child was—the Saviour from God. We need to remember that there had been many who had born the name of "Jesus" already. This is the Greek name or form of the common Hebrew name "Joshua." The first Joshua of whom we read was called originally Oshea or Hoshea; this name, which was also the name of the last king of Israel and of the first in order of the minor prophets, means "salvation." But Joshua and all of the others of like name were dependent upon Jehovah to bring salvation. Now Jesus is born, and His name is Emmanuel, "God with us." The angel reminded Joseph that "he shall save his people from their sins." He, of himself is able to save His people from their sins, for He is God, dwelling among men. He came to redeem us all and to "purify unto himself a peculiar people, zealous of good works" (Titus 2:14).

Joshua led the Children of Israel over into the Promised Land, but the Lord Jesus is leading His children into the eternal city, where He has gone to prepare a home for those who receive Him as their Saviour.

There is a sacred meaning to the name of Jesus. We ought to face the fact that He is saving men from their sins today, and that He is ready to save everyone who will trust in Him. We ought also to face the reality that this name is a holy name, and we should not use it carelessly. We are reminded to trust in the person of that name and to approach the very throne room of God in the name of Jesus.

3

Matthew 2:1-23

~~~~~~

The Childhood of Jesus

THE CHAPTER OUTLINED:

I. The Coming of the Wise Men (Matt. 2:1-12)
   The Arrival of the Wise Men (vv. 9-11)
II. The Flight into Egypt (Matt. 2:13-14)
III. The Massacre of the Children at Bethlehem (Matt. 2:16-18)
IV. The Return to Nazareth (Matt. 2:19-23)
V. The Years in Nazareth
   (a)   His hometown—Nazareth
   (b)   His schooling
   (c)   His early labor
   (d)   His early travels

INTRODUCTION

There has never been any birth of any child as significant as the birth of Jesus. No birth has been so widely and continuously celebrated, nor has any birth had so great an influence upon the history of mankind as the birth of Jesus. Heaven was moved to send angels to announce it. The sky bore witness to it by the presence of a particular star sent to guide the Wise Men who came from the East bearing gifts for the King. Herod was moved to an action determined to kill the child; and Joseph and his family, Mary and the Babe, fled to escape this awful deed of murder. All of this unfolds in this portion of our study.

THE EXPOSITION

The story of the visit of the Wise Men and the subsequent reactions are recorded only by Matthew. There are three movements of the early childhood of Jesus recorded here, and in only one other place do we have a Biblical record of His early days—read Luke 2.

I. The Coming of the Wise Men (Matt. 2:1-12)

This section raises many questions—some which we would ask, others which were asked by those who came. The first is very simple: Who were the Wise Men? (v. 1). The phrase translated "wise men" is one simple Greek word, *magi*. We get our words "magic" and "magician" from this word. But these men were not magicians in the modern sense. They were perhaps men of unusual wisdom, attending the kings of Babylon and Persia. They appear frequently, for example, in the Book of Daniel (2:12; 5:11; also I Kings 4:30-31). We do discover some men referred to by this title in the Book of the Acts, but for the most part they were imposters, still in attendance upon officials in the Roman government, but given to various tricks and to the practices of occultism (cf. Acts 13:6).

The second question is one raised by these men themselves, in Matthew 2:2, when they asked, "Where is he that is born King of the Jews?" This is a very significant question, for it identifies the Lord Jesus with the kingship of the Jews. Isaiah had prophesied many years before that "the government shall be upon his shoulder. . . . Of the increase of his government, and peace there shall be no end, upon the throne of David, and upon his kingdom, to order it, and to establish it. . . . The zeal of the Lord of hosts will perform this" (Isa. 9:6-7).

The third question that comes to us concerns the star that guided them. The Wise Men simply said, "for we have seen this star in the east, and are come to worship him." What do we know about the star? Was it a special star? Did it shine more brightly than any other star? This star is and has been the subject of a vast amount of literature, and yet we still know very little about it in any specific way. I am convinced that we may know for a surety that it was placed in the heavens for the specific occasion which is now under our study. But there is another question raised, which is: How could these men know that this star would lead them to the King for whom they were searching? The Bible does not give us this answer. However, indications are that they were familiar with the Old Testament, and particularly the Book of Daniel, where there is a timetable, telling us the time of the incarnation of the Lord Jesus (cf. Dan. 9:25).

The Wise Men then tell their reason for coming, "and are come to worship him" (v. 2). Dr. Wilbur Smith once commented on this passage that those who give themselves to the pursuit of wisdom are never fully satisfied with the wisdom this earth provides. These Wise Men came seeking Christ, because they felt there was something lacking in their knowledge, an element that was beyond their wisdom. The Apostle Paul reminds us that, "In . . . [Christ] are hid all the treasures of wisdom and knowledge" (Col. 2:3). Men who know Jesus as their Lord are wise beyond the wisdom of this world and find complete satisfaction in Him. Men who do not know

Christ, even though they be listed among this world's greatest intellects, are still in darkness, and can be found seeking satisfaction in numerous realms of life.

The coming of the Wise Men brought a reaction from the king, and this is of such vital importance that Matthew, under the direction of the Holy Spirit, records it in his book (vv. 3-8). We need to identify this king, for there are three Herods occupying places of significance in the New Testament. Each one of them is identified with attempts to destroy Christ and the Christian faith. One Herod occupied the throne at the time of the birth of Christ, but died shortly after His birth; Herod Antipas, the son of this Herod, who ordered John the Baptist put to death, and before whom Jesus stood at the time of His trial; and Herod Agrippa, the grandson, before whom the Apostle Paul stood in defense of his life. The Herod, on the throne at the time of Christ's birth, was appointed king by the Roman Senate, 40 B.C. He besieged and took Jerusalem in 37 B.C. Knowing that his power was wrapped up in Rome, he took every opportunity to maintain goodwill with the politicians of Rome. The text tells us that "he was troubled" due to the presence and questions of the Wise Men. He recognized that he had no legal or regal reason for his appointment as "king." It was purely political, and this scared him.

The phrase "and all Jerusalem with him," is an exciting phrase. The questions of the Wise Men must have gotten around fast, and the city began to buzz with conversation. This would be especially true among the political figures of the city. Herod went immediately to the religious leaders (v. 4) and inquired of them "where the Christ should be born." It is extremely interesting that without consultation they immediately responded, "In Bethlehem of Judaea," and then quoted from Micah 5:2. These religious leaders knew the prophecy. That Micah was referring to the Messiah cannot be questioned, for these leaders of the Jews quoted it immediately. It was well known by Jews for hundreds of years before Jesus was born. Though these religious leaders knew of the promise of God, they were not excited enough to go down to Bethlehem when they heard these Wise Men from the East declare that the King was born. They knew the Scriptures, but failed to accept them or to act upon them. What a word of application for our own hearts today. Many who know the truth fail to act upon it. The indifference they showed at this time later erupted into actual hatred that led them to demand that Jesus be put to death.

Now Herod talks with the Wise Men privately. He had learned that the King was to be born in Bethlehem and now he is desirous of more information; therefore, he "enquired of them diligently what time the star appeared" (v. 7). Without doubt the plot to destroy the babe was already taking shape in his mind. He must go back long enough to make sure that his edict would include that much time. He sent the Wise Men on their way with specific instruction that when they had found the child they were to "bring me word again, that I may come and worship him also" (v. 8). There can be no question but that these words are words of deceit. He had no intention of worshiping; rather, he wanted to determine where the child might be, in order to rid himself of the threat of another who would take his throne.

The Arrival of the Wise Men (vv. 9-11). The Wise Men left the king, and once again they saw the star, which they had first observed in the East. Matthew reminds us that the star "went before them, till it came and stood over where the young child was." These men did not stop short of their goal. They inquired, got answers, then followed directions both of the informants and the star. Verse 10 reminds us that "when they saw the star, they rejoiced with exceeding great joy." It is not without basis that the time we celebrate, even today, as the birthday of the Lord should bring with it so much joy. It began on that note and continues to the present hour. Read the account in full from both of these Gospels, Matthew and Luke, and you catch this note of joy from the pen of each writer. The coming of Jesus into the world meant redemption for mankind; it showed forth the love of God toward His creatures.

Now there is a change in the language. The birth had taken place in a manger, but in verse 11 we note that the Wise Men came "into the house." There in the manger, it was the baby Jesus, but now they worshiped "the young child." Apparently, it was some time after the birth. Scripture is silent on the elapsed time element, although it is specific on the change of place. The crowds that had come for the registration, without doubt, had returned to their homes, and Joseph and Mary moved into a house. We are certain of one thing, the Wise Men found them—"and when they were come into the house, they saw the young child with Mary his mother, and they fell down, and worshipped him" (v. 11). The Scriptures never hint that worship was meant for Mary; often, in later years, we discover men who worshiped Jesus, even as the Wise Men did on this occasion.

The word "worship" here means "to touch the ground with the forehead." As a part of their worship, they presented "treasures." This is a word which we use in our own language, "thesaurus" for a collection of words. It carries with it the idea that out of their collection of things, which were carried in a box, or jewel box, they gave certain gifts— "gold, and frankincense, and myrrh." There are many suggestive thoughts attached to these three gifts. For example: the gold—representing deity; the frankincense—the sweetest of all odors—was offered to the Son of God, who as God was due the sweetest sacrifice of prayer; and the myrrh—to Jesus, the Son of mankind, who now as man has made Himself subject to mortality. The myrrh carrying with it the significance that though He would die, yet He would not see corruption. Myrrh is often used as an embalming fluid in the Holy Land.

The very fact that three gifts are mentioned, has caused some to believe that there were three Wise Men, but this number is nowhere stated in the Scripture. The last word we read regarding the Wise Men is that they were warned in a dream by God that they should not return to Jerusalem and the palace of Herod, but that they should go home by another route. This they did, and their part of the story is ended.

II. The Flight into Egypt (Matt. 2:13-14)

Now, Joseph had another visit from an angel; this time to warn Joseph to take Mary and the young child "and flee into Egypt, and be thou there until I bring thee word." We do not know how long Joseph and the family remained in Egypt, we only know that they went there in obedience to the voice of God through the angel. It may have been several weeks, or months, or even years. God told Joseph the reason for the direction, "for Herod will seek the young child to destroy him" (v. 13). God never asks any of us to do anything without a reason for the direction. Matthew adds to the statement of fact that this, too, is a fulfillment of prophecy (v. 15; cf. Hosea 11:1) which refers to Israel the people, but is legitimately transferred to Christ, in whom Israel is summed up.

III. The Massacre of the Children at Bethlehem (Matt. 2:16-18)

Many question the truth of this story, because of the silence of Josephus on the subject. The writer of our book, Matthew, reported it as historical fact, and that is sufficient. Dr. Laird has written concerning this: "The deed illustrates well Herod's general character for bloodthirsty cruelty and shortsighted folly. But all his efforts to defeat the purposes of God which He had declared in the beginning of the nation, turn out to be shortsighted folly." Joseph, warned in a dream by the angel, took Mary and the young child and hastily moved to Egypt where they could wait further direction from God. Let us remember that God could have performed a miracle and removed Herod from the scene of action immediately, but He did not thus plan nor perform it. Jesus must go to Egypt, to be called back after a while in fulfillment of the prophetic Word "Out of Egypt have I called my son." This prophecy is found in Hosea 11:1, and was spoken about 700 years prior to the time of the flight of Jesus to Egypt. The promise itself was about Israel, but the Holy Spirit interpreted its complete fulfillment to Matthew, and reminds us that it refers to Jesus, the Son of Man, who is the firstborn from the dead (cf. Exod. 4:22; and Jer. 31:9).

In the next three verses (Matt. 2:16-18) we see something of the anger of Herod when he finds out that the Wise Men did not return as he had asked them to do. Immediately, he had all the boys in Bethlehem and in all its borders from two years and under killed. This, Matthew reminds us, is the fulfillment of that which was spoken by Jeremiah the prophet, saying: "A voice was heard in Ramah, lamentation, and bitter weeping; Rahel weeping for her children refused to be comforted for her children, because they were not" (Jer. 31:15).

IV. The Return to Nazareth (Matt. 2:19-23)

We are reminded in verse 23, of yet another prophecy which is now fulfilled. Archelaus succeeded as king of Judaea and Samaria. He was noted for his cruelty and misgovernment, and was finally banished to Gaul. The important part of the return of Joseph and the family of Jesus is that they came and "dwelt in a city called Nazareth: that it might be fulfilled which was spoken by the prophets, He shall be called a Nazarene." Note, it does not say that the words were spoken by a *prophet*, but the word is plural—prophets. Many of the prophets had spoken of Jesus as being a Nazarene. A Nazarene is an inhabitant of Nazareth. That city is in Galilee, which is called the Galilee of the Gentiles because so many Gentiles lived there. The Pharisees and scribes in Jerusalem hated and despised Galilee, and especially was Nazareth despised. Even the Galileans looked down upon the town and despised everybody who lived there. This was a part of the reason for the question of Nathanael who said, "Can there any good thing come out of Nazareth?" (John 1:46). Jesus had come to be the Saviour of men, but before that could happen, He must die. His death began with His rejection, and that began in Nazareth where He spent the early days of His life.

V. The Years in Nazareth

Although not too much is said concerning these years spent in Nazareth, there are some implications from the Bible which deserve a bit of our attention.

After the return from Egypt very little is known of His life. Chapter 2 closes with the simple statement that He "came and dwelt in a city called Nazareth." We do not know when He returned, except that we may assume that it was after He was two years of age; because the decree was that all the male children two years and under should be put to death. Since nothing is said concerning Joseph after the visit to the Temple (Luke 2:42-52), many assume that he died. This idea is at least strengthened by the fact that Jesus committed the care of Mary to John at the time of the crucifixion.

However, there are some things implied in the facts we have that help to provide interesting sidelights into the preparation for the ministry of the earthly life of Jesus. We need to remember that in childhood there is a foundation laid for the future work of life.

(a) **His hometown—Nazareth.** It was not a large city, but Nazareth was known as a notoriously wicked town. Here Jesus came into contact with various types of activity, with both good and bad people in the eyes of the world. There is a lesson here for us, that even in the midst of a very sinful generation and a wicked city, it is possible to have a godly home and from it issue forth good life! In Jesus' case, it remained a "spotless life." His home training must have been in an excellent spiritual atmosphere, full of love, purity and good morals. Dr. Luke reminds us that "he [Jesus] went down with them, and came to Nazareth, and was subject unto them" (Luke 2:51).

(b) **His schooling.** In Nazareth, as in any of the cities of

Palestine in that day, the major schools taught largely from the Scriptures. Dr. Stalker reminds us that Jesus knew three languages: Hebrew, for His quotations were from the Hebrew; Aramaic, which was the common language of the people; and Greek, since there were many Greek-speaking inhabitants in the city. We are convinced that Jesus had an excellent schooling, for when He returned to His own country the natives began to question "what wisdom is this which is given unto him" (Matt. 13:54-58, Mark 6:2-6). In the Scripture we remember also that the history of the Jews was opened to him as a lad.

(c) **His early labor.** Another important part of His childhood training was that of His business training. He learned the trade of a carpenter, and Mark tells us that He worked at this occupation (Mark 6:3). Man must work to earn his livelihood, and it is wonderful to know that our Saviour was disciplined in daily work, thus learning by experience the testings of the laborer. It is in the school of business that we learn many of the lessons that prepare us for useful living.

(d) **His early travels.** We hear much in our own generation to the effect that travel is a very important part of an education. One item of which we are sure, although it is only mentioned casually, is that the Lord Jesus traveled much to and from Nazareth to Jerusalem. Those who know it best, tell us that the scenery of this part of the world is among the "most beautiful on the face of the earth." Out of these experiences Jesus was able to draw many illustrations and teachings.

Thus, although the Bible record is scarce concerning His childhood, we can discern that these things all were a part of God's program of preparation for the work that Jesus had come to fulfill.

4

Matthew 3:1–4:25

━━━━━━━━━━━━━━━━━━━━━━━━━━

The Preparation and Initiation of Jesus into His Ministry

THE CHAPTER OUTLINED:

INTRODUCTION
THE EXPOSITION
I. The Preparatory Ministry of John the Baptist (Matt. 3:1-12)
   1. The instrument God used (v. 1)
   2. The locality in which he ministered (v. 1)
   3. The message he preached (vv. 2-12)
   4. The purpose of his preaching (v. 3)
   5. The baptism he performed (vv. 6, 11)
   6. The condemnation of John toward the Pharisees and Sadducees (vv. 7-10)
   7. The announcement of the King (vv. 11-12)
II. Preparation and Initiation through Baptism (Matt. 3:13-17)
III. Preparation and Initiation through Temptation (Matt. 4:1-11)
   1. Led by the Spirit
   2. "Tempted"
   3. He was tempted "of the devil" (v. 1)
   4. He fasted and became hungry (v. 2)
   5. The first temptation—physical (vv. 3-4)
   6. The second temptation—presumption (vv. 5-7)
   7. The third temptation—to rebel (vv. 8-11)
IV. The Beginning of His Public Ministry (Matt. 4:12-17)

INTRODUCTION

In the study of the life of Christ as recorded by Matthew, it is important that we see each portion as a part of the whole pattern. The movement in this section is very rapid, although many days are included in the actual performance of Christ.

EXPOSITION

Here we are introduced to the ministry of John the Baptist, including the baptism of the Lord, which actually becomes the climactic time of John's ministry. John was the forerunner of the Lord as he came to "prepare the way of the Lord." It was John's privilege to announce and introduce Jesus as "the Lamb of God, which taketh away the sin of the world" (John 1:29).

I. The Preparatory Ministry of John the Baptist (Matt. 3:1-12)

John the Baptist was born in the hill country of Judaea, about six months before the birth of Jesus. His parents were Zacharias, the priest, and his wife, Elizabeth, who was the cousin of Mary. This means that John was the child of prayer and prophecy. He was a Nazarite, drinking "neither wine nor strong drink; and he . . . [was] filled with the Holy Ghost, even from his mother's womb" (Luke 1:15). His early years are summed up in one verse of Scripture (Luke 1:80), where we discover that He grew physically and became strong in spirit. He had keen spiritual insight and this period of preparation gave him opportunity to have deep communion with God.

1. The instrument God used (v. 1). John, being the son of Zacharias, the priest, is a part of the priestly line. Although John did not minister in the Temple, he had a priestly ministry. His very birth was unusual due to the advanced age of his parents. God had a special ministry for him to perform, hence, raised him at a particular time.

2. The locality in which he ministered (v. 1). It was in the wilderness of Judaea, along the Jordan River. The word "wilderness" simply means a sparsely populated section. Without doubt in the beginning his audiences were small, but grew as the fame of his preaching spread.

3. **The message he preached (vv. 2-12).** John's message was an indictment of sin. Its theme was that of repentance, and this he urged upon all men regardless of rank or position. The reason, he cited, was simply that God was about to reveal the promised Messiah, and the nation should prepare for the event through repentance. Although John does not reveal much of the condition of his times, the unfolding of the story and his subsequent death reveal the presence of moral debauchery and a low level of spiritual standards. It points up the reality that when those who are in high places set the standards for their own lives at a low level, the people in general will follow. John preached repentance in very clear as well as severe language without respect of the people in his audience. He preached against the sins of the people in order to bring conviction to their hearts. He preached the coming judgment of God (vv. 7, 10).

4. **The purpose of his preaching (v. 3).** The total purpose of his ministry is wrapped up in the statement of Matthew, which includes a portion from the prophet Isaiah: "Prepare ye the way of the Lord, make his paths straight" (v. 3; cf. Isa. 40:3).

5. **The baptism he performed (vv. 6, 11).** We need to be very clear at this point and emphasize that Christian baptism is not being taught in this chapter. Much error has come because many try to use this as a proof text for Christian baptism. There are sufficient texts that do teach Christian baptism, but this is not one of them. The people came out of various places to hear John preach repentance; and as they came, they were convicted of their sins, confessed those sins, and went down into the waters of baptism—"John's Baptism," which is tied to their repentance. A clear understanding of this will help in an understanding of Acts 19:2-5. Jews who had been baptized with John's baptism (Acts 19:3) were now

baptized with Christian baptism (Acts 19:5) after they understood the difference. Paul reminds us that John's baptism was the "baptism of repentance" (Acts 19:4). Christian baptism is not a "baptism unto repentance," but rather, it is unto Christ's death and resurrection (Rom. 6:3-5).

6. The condemnation of John toward the Pharisees and Sadducees (vv. 7-10). We are introduced for the first time in this book to two prominent religious classes and leaders among the Jews; the Pharisees and the Sadducees. These two classes are to play an important role in the book we study; therefore, a review of their tenets will be helpful.

The Pharisees were those who by their very name, "Pharisees"—which means "separatist," claimed to be "holier than thou." They were the strictly religious, orthodox, ritualistic class. They were well versed in the traditions of the elders and occupied themselves with creating new commandments and strange interpretations of the law. They are in essence the fathers of the Talmudical Jews of the present day and typical of ritualistic Christendom; having the form of godliness but denying the power of it.

The Sadducees were the rationalists, the unbelieving class. They were much given to reform, and they have their counterpart today among the reformed Jews. They rejected the greater part of the Word of God. In modern Christendom today they have to a degree reproduced themselves in the neo-evangelicals, who though they call themselves Christians, reject portions of the Word and do not believe in any form of verbal inspiration of the Word. John, in his denunciation, reminds them that they are the offspring of vipers. They believed they were to be saved from the wrath of God by the establishment of the kingdom and that the wrath would fall entirely upon Gentile nations. John demands that they produce fruit worthy of repentance. He uncovers their false pretenses and shows that no natural birth nor religious attainment would deliver them in the day of wrath. This is followed by the announcement of the nearness of the judgment, the axe laid at the root of the trees, ready to fell the mighty trees void of fruit.

7. The announcement of the King (vv. 11-12). John baptized with water, the symbol and means of outward cleansing; but "he that cometh after me," referring to Jesus, "shall baptize you with the Holy Ghost, and with fire." What John here announced and proclaimed was entirely prophetic; it blended together the first and second comings of Christ. At the death, resurrection, ascension, and glorification of Christ, the Holy Spirit was given to those who believed on Christ; that is, they were baptized by the Holy Spirit, into one Body, the Church. From that moment on, all who receive Him as Saviour are "in the Spirit" as to their life and sphere. They are baptized into one Body, the Body of the risen and glorified Lord (cf. Eph. 1:19-23). The fire baptism will take place when the Lord returns to the earth the second time; it is a baptism of judgment upon the unbelieving (notice v. 12 — "gather his wheat into the garner; but he will burn up the chaff with unquenchable fire").

II. Preparation and Initiation through Baptism (Matt. 3:13-17)

The moment has arrived, and the ministry of John the Baptist is being terminated. It has brought us step by step to this moment. John the Baptist never allowed himself to become the center of attraction. He had preached of one who should come, and now the moment of introduction has come. At first, John stood in amazement, actually trying to hinder Jesus from being baptized. He declared, "I have need to be baptized of thee, and comest thou to me?" In other words, John is saying—I am the sinner, I am the one standing in need of repentance, I deserve to go into the water, but Thou art holy—no evil in Thee, nothing worthy of repentance. However, Jesus insisted, saying that He must be baptized "to fulfill all righteousness" (v. 15).

Much controversy has arisen over Christ's baptism. But He has given the answer to the controversy. He did not need to repent and obtain remission for sins, for He had none. He did come, and now identifies himself with a sinful human race by this act. He actually got under the load of sin that He might lift it from men, for He had come to "save his people from their sins" (Matt. 1:21). In this testimony from the lips of John, we have testimony of His holiness. He is the One who alone is holy, harmless, undefiled, separate from sinners. He was baptized that He might fulfill the righteousness demanded. Notice, there was no confessing or repenting of sin on His part, but He must be identified with them for whom He had come to save.

As He came up out of the water, heaven was opened and the Holy Spirit descended "like a dove" upon the Son of God. We are not told definitely that the multitude saw this manifestation of the Spirit, but we dare to at least infer that they did. This was a visible introduction of Christ from heaven. We still believe in teaching by visuals, and here is an illustration of one. We dare not stay at the point of the symbolism of the dove as a type or picture of the Holy Spirit. But we are reminded of the dove which flew across the waters of Noah's day, at first finding no resting place, but when sent out a second time returning with an olive branch and the third time "no return." Now, the dove as the picture of the Holy Spirit, comes to abide upon the life of Christ, who later promised that the Holy Spirit would come upon all believers, and would be their "paraclete."

But there was more—there was an audible introduction of Christ. After the coming of the Holy Spirit, there was a voice heard from heaven. If those watching had thought they were being victimized with an illusion when they saw the dove, their fears were dispelled by the voice. The Father acknowledged Jesus as His Son and He also expressed His delight in Him. Jesus had come to do the Father's will, and His baptism was the indication that He would fulfill all of it. He had identified himself with the sinful race of men that were in need of salvation. His whole career from this time onward sets forth His purpose to be the Saviour of men. In this baptism we have a manifestation of the Triune God: the Son was baptized, the Spirit descended upon Him, and the voice of the Father was heard from heaven.

III. Preparation and Initiation through Temptation (Matt. 4: 1-11)

As a further step in the introduction of Jesus to His ministry, we discover a time of temptation. The Father had already put His stamp of approval on the Son, knowing before the testing by Satan, that Jesus could and would bear the testing and remain unmoved. Actually, the Father's approval of Christ was a challenge to the accuser.

1. Led by the Spirit. Matthew calls attention to the fact that Jesus was "led up of the spirit into the wilderness to be tempted of the devil" (v. 1). In rehearsing this story, Mark, the author of the Book of Mark, uses a stronger word that is translated "driveth" (Mark 1:12). This word indicates the use of force or forceful persuasion. It says to us that Jesus did not of His own will rush into the place of testing, but He was led up of the Holy Spirit who had come upon Him at His baptism.

2. "Tempted." This word has the sense and meaning "to stretch out, to try the strength of." When used in a bad sense, it means "to entice, solicit, or provoke to sin." Why was Christ tempted? Was it to see if He would be true or if He would fail under such severe testing? We are convinced this cannot be true. God the Father knew His Son would not fail, but that He would remain absolutely true to the Father's holy will and purpose. As the Son of God, He is now to be tested as to obedience to the Father and dependence upon Him. This testing took place in order to demonstrate to the world the fact that indeed He was the Son of God, sinless and holy, therefore, able and equipped to do the work He had come into the world to do. For this purpose the Holy Spirit impelled Jesus to go into the wilderness. Someone has suggested that "the first Adam was tempted in a garden; the last Adam in a wilderness; the first Adam when tempted was surrounded by plenty; the last Adam by desolation."

3. He was tempted "of the devil" (v. 1). His temptation came from without; it was a testing. It was not solicitation to sin of His own lust or desire (cf. James 1:13-15). Jesus had no sin in Him; He was sinless. His human nature as well as His divine nature was sinless (cf. Heb. 4:15). The temptation of Jesus was from the devil—he was and is a real person. He is just as real as Jesus is real, not as some would indicate, a mere influence of evil.

4. He fasted and became hungry (v. 2). Matthew tells us very simply that He fasted 40 days; while Luke (4:2) describes the situation by saying, "he did eat nothing." Being tested for 40 days, even though abstaining from food, Jesus was miraculously sustained, for ordinarily to go without food for 40 days would leave one in a very weakened condition. Then Matthew adds, "he was afterward an hungered." To know that Jesus was hungry is proof that He suffered physical appetites even as we. During the 40 days there were temptations, but 3 now are detailed in the climax of them all.

5. The first temptation—physical (vv. 3-4). The devil assaulted Jesus in His natural want and appealed to Him to exercise His power to relieve His want, and thus by miracle, to demonstrate that He was the Son of God. This was a very subtle testing. The need of Jesus was real, the hunger perfectly natural and sinless, and He possessed the power to relieve himself. Why then should He not do so? The answer is obvious: Because in so doing He would have cast a doubt upon the words of His Father and failed in the path of obedience to His Father. He would have been yielding to His own will and would thus have taken the case into His own hands. Notice, He did not argue with Satan, but resisted him instantly and uncompromisingly. He quoted from Deuteronomy 8:3, and so met the word of the devil by His Father's Word.

6. The second temptation—presumption (vv. 5-7). The first temptation finds the devil defeated, but not giving up. Very carefully, he turned Christ's previous reply into a fresh means of attack. It is as if he implied in his temptation that since Jesus is depending upon God, He should depend on Him to the limit. Let Him cast himself down from the pinnacle of the Temple. The pinnacle of the Temple literally is the wing of the Temple. The devil at this point changed his method of attack. Jesus had quoted the Word of God in the devil's first attempt, so now the devil quotes from the Scriptures. He quoted Psalm 91:11-12 which is a Messianic Psalm. But in doing so, he left out a clause, namely, "to keep thee in all thy ways." The very words the devil left out are words that guard against the abuse of this promise of protection. Here again, the devil tempted Jesus, this time to presumption. The devil tempted Jesus to choose His own will and not the will of the Father, by acting in presumption. Here is a very practical truth for all who follow Jesus—be sure to guard against misuse of the Word of God. It is so easy to take the Scriptures out of their context, and thus to give a misinterpretation to that which has been written for our blessing. Once again, Jesus met the temptation by quoting from the Word of God, using Deuteronomy 6:16. He stood true not only to the truth of the Word, but to its proper interpretation. He did not presume.

7. The third temptation—to rebel (vv. 8-11). Satan has not changed his objective of getting Jesus to submit to temptation, but once again the devil changes the method. He took Jesus upon a high mountain and showed Him all the kingdoms of the world and their glory. The devil knew that Jesus was the heir to all the kingdoms of the world, but now he offers them to Him if He would but give homage to him. What an offer! Do not think this impossible, for the Lord Himself often called Satan "the prince of this world" (cf. John 12:31; 14:30; 16:11). He was offering the world kingdoms to Jesus by a road other than the way of the Cross.

In each of these three it is obvious that Satan's one desire was to keep Jesus from doing the will of the Father, but Jesus refused to listen to the tempter. Once again, in meeting the temptation, Jesus quoted from the Scriptures (Deut. 6:13) and commanded Satan to leave.

One thing is evident in all of these testings of our Lord: He never displayed His deity nor did He use His divine power. Though it was suggested by Satan, Jesus never bowed to the desire of Satan; but rather, He conquered the devil with the simple use of the Word of God. How practical a lesson for everyone who follows Jesus Christ. But that means that we must know what the Scriptures say and how to apply them. Then it is possible for everyone of us to defeat the devil.

These truths seem extremely important to us in a day when "Satan's Church" is actually gaining popularity in some segments of American society. Not many will publicly declare themselves to be a part of this church, but even in churches dedicated to the worship of Christ, there are many who in strange ways are succumbing to the kind of thing Satan tried to get the Lord to do.

IV. The Beginning of His Public Ministry (Matt. 4:12-17)

It is quite evident that between verses 11 and 12, there is a time gap. From the writers of other Gospels, we discover that Jesus went back to the place where John the Baptist was ministering. John especially records something of that return in 1:29 where we read, "The next day"; and again on two days following he records truth concerning Jesus (vv. 30, 43). On that first occasion Jesus seems to have lingered in the crowd, unrecognized except by John the Baptist. The next day Jesus moved toward John, and then John made the great announcement concerning the Lamb of God that would take away the sin of the world. The following day he announced it again, but this time, only: "Behold the Lamb of God"—and by this statement he lost two disciples.

There followed an elapse of time until John the Baptist

was arrested. Although some important things take place, Matthew does not include them in his record. Jesus and His first followers went to Cana of Galilee, then to Capernaum, and on to Jerusalem, where Jesus went into the Temple and cleansed it.

Matthew picks up the story of Jesus as the Messiah-King after John the Baptist has been silenced. Jesus now begins to preach and teach. Three things we notice in this paragraph. (a) Jesus came down into Capernaum and took up His residence there and began to preach: "Repent, for the kingdom of heaven is at hand." (b) Then He began to gather a group of followers who would help with His labors. (c) The final verses tell us a bit of the success He had in this early ministry. Matthew reminds us that Jesus' going to Capernaum is so that Isaiah's prophecy might be fulfilled. As Christ called men to follow Him, it was a call to the abandonment of the old ways of life, to a new way of service.

The closing paragraph (vv. 23-25), tells of our Lord's ministry in Galilee, as He went about that country, teaching, preaching and healing. This brought much fame throughout Syria, and the multitudes flocked to see and hear Him.

5

Matthew 5:1–7:29

~~~~~~~~~~~~~~~~~~~~~~~~~~~~~~~~~~~~~~~

The Teaching of the King Concerning the Kingdom

THE CHAPTER OUTLINED:

INTRODUCTION
THE EXPOSITION
  I.   Laws in Relationship to Our Fellow Men (Matt. 5)
       (a) The introduction (vv. 1-2)
       (b) The Beatitudes (vv. 3-12)
            1. "The poor in spirit" (v. 3)
            2. "They that mourn" (v. 4)
            3. "The meek" are mentioned next (v. 5)
            4. The hungry and thirsty man (v. 6)
            5. "The merciful" (v. 7)
            6. "The pure in heart" (v. 8)
            7. "The peacemakers" (v. 9)
       (c) The effects of true Christianity (vv. 13-16)
       (d) True righteousness identified (vv. 17-48)
            1. The true significance of the law (vv. 17-20)
               The law of murder (vv. 21-26)
               The law of adultery (vv. 27-30)
 II.   Our Relationship with God (Matt. 6)
       1. Right motives (6:1-18)
       2. Right attitudes (vv. 19-34)
III.   Direction Concerning Needs—Encouragement and Warnings
       (Matt. 7)
       1. Judgments (vv. 1-6)
       2. Prayer (vv. 7-12)
       3. Two roads, to gates (vv. 13-22)
       4. False teachers and their fruits (vv. 15-23)
       5. Building and its results (vv. 24-27)

INTRODUCTION

The three chapters which form our text are often referred to as the "Sermon on the Mount," which name is taken from the fact that Matthew tells us "he went up into a mountain . . . and taught them."

Chapter 4 of Matthew closed on the note of great multitudes following Jesus. This one begins—"and seeing the multitudes." The contents of the three chapters involved are in the form of a continuing message which is found in no other section of the New Testament. There are some portions of Luke's Gospel which are similar in nature, but they are in entirely different settings and there are also other variations. We can only conclude, therefore, that these recorded events are not two records of the same incident, but rather of similar occasions. Matthew alone gives us the text of the so-called Sermon on the Mount.

In order to get a proper background for our study it seems imperative to begin by clearly correcting three false impressions or interpretations which are common in Christendom today.

(a) That the Sermon on the Mount reveals the way of salvation and the development of the human race for which the world of men should strive. To correct this error, you are reminded that the teaching of this passage was directed to the disciples, and the message speaks of the characteristics of those who have been redeemed. There is no salvation mentioned; the way a sinner is saved is not revealed here. If it is a gospel (good news), it then is a gospel of good works, of doing good, of improving oneself. This, the Bible clearly denies as an act of man. It is impossible for sinful men to save themselves.

(b) That the Sermon on the Mount is strictly for the church, and the application is strictly Christian. If the Lord had the church in mind, the lesson should have been taught after His announcement of the church, as found in Matthew 16:13 and following. Suffice it to say that this section under study is not the direction given to the church. That direction is particularly given by the Apostle Paul in his letters to the churches. If this lesson is applied in its strictest sense to the church, then we will be entangled in a legal bondage as great as that of the Pharisees.

(c) The third false interpretation makes these Scriptures exclusively Jewish. There are those who refuse to accept that this section has any reference to Christian believers; hence, Christians can eliminate the application from all consideration in their lives. This is equally as wrong as the error of the previous paragraph.

The Sermon on the Mount was the proclamation of the King concerning His kingdom. It has reference to the millennial earth and the kingdom Christ will establish upon the earth. However, it does not exclude application to believers who are members of His body and who will share His heavenly throne with Him in the heavenly Jerusalem. The kingdom has a heavenly and an earthly side, both of which are seen here.

THE EXPOSITION

There are many suggestions as to how we might divide this section, but because of the vast amount of material, and to enable us to get the overall view, we are dividing the material into three sections that correspond to the chapter divisions of the King James Version: Chapter 5 gives us the laws that are to be obeyed in relationship with our fellow men; Chapter 6 is primarily the laws concerning our relationship with or to God; and Chapter 7 in which Jesus sets forth some needs, some encouragements, and finally some warnings.

I. Laws in Relationship to Our Fellow Men (Matt. 5)

The fifth chapter begins with the setting forth of the Beatitudes which many of us have memorized early in life. The great need to understand and apply now becomes the essential.

(a) The introduction (vv. 1-2). Every word of the Bible is important, but these first two verses seem especially important. Already, great multitudes were continually crowding around Jesus, to catch the words of wisdom they knew would come from His lips. The mountain from which He spoke is unnamed, hence we leave it just as it is. The word translated "disciples," means "learners" as over against "teachers." History tells us that after the ascension, this term was generally applied to all who had embraced the Christian faith.

(b) **The Beatitudes (vv. 3-12).** As we begin the study of these verses, we want to give some consideration to the word "blessed" which appears at the beginning of each of these Beatitudes. Some say that its best meaning is that of "happy," but in our present day this word suggests lightheartedness, superficiality. Blessedness is deeper; it is a matter of character. The original word was used in classical Greek by poets and philosophers for the attainment of life's ideal, the *summum bonum*, greatest good. The word from the original is translated in our Authorized Version as "blessed" 43 times, and as "happy" 6 times. It would seem that the two cannot be separated. Happiness is God's will for man—but we must likewise understand that blessed implies divine grace which is bestowed upon the obedient Christ-like disciple. Someone once said, "Happiness is heat reflected from without. Blessedness is a fire within that sheds light and warmth whatever the weather outside."

Now the Lord indicates who are the blessed and tells of their rewards.

(1) **"The poor in spirit" (v. 3).** This phrase indicates utter destitution. It is the opposite of pride, self-righteousness, self-conceit. It is possible for men to be proud of their wealth, but likewise it is possible that men are proud of their poverty, or for a praying man to be proud of his supplications, for the fasting to be proud of his fasts, or the giver of gifts to be proud of his giving. But Jesus here wipes it all away! The reward—"their's is the kingdom of heaven." It is not something gained by being poor in spirit, but rather, this is a mark of the Christian character.

(2) "They that mourn" (v. 4). Jesus does not describe the mourning, but includes all mourning—whether it be over sorrow brought about by human suffering, or spiritual sorrow brought about by the sin and ignorance of the man himself, over his own sin, or over the sins of those about him. Sorrow—as we see the sins and needs of the world which even now is lying in wickedness. Their reward—"they shall be comforted." This promise reminds us of the Holy Spirit—our Comforter, the ever-present help. As sorrow draws men to God, they may be sure that this sorrow will bring comfort from the very heart of God.

(3) "The meek" are mentioned next (v. 5). Meekness is popularly confused with weakness and the present-day Mr. Milquetoast—for he has become the world's symbol for a meek person. However, this is contrary to the teaching of the Scriptures; and here, it is simply the "Awareness of our own littleness in the light of God's greatness." When a man sees himself like this, he does not insist upon his own rights. He is satisfied to inherit the place God gives him in that kingdom where righteousness will dwell forever.

(4) The hungry and thirsty man (v. 6). Not all hungering and thirsting will make a man a blessed man. Desire for that which does not satisfy results in disappointment and will leave one with a spiritual void. The desire Jesus speaks of here is that of earnestly seeking righteousness, and God's promise is that it shall be ours, completely and permanently.

(5) "The merciful" (v. 7). When men see the needs of those round about and seek to minister to those needs, they are in turn promised God's mercy.

(6) "The pure in heart" (v. 8). Here is the basic difference between Old Testament law and New Testament law. The law centered attention on outward acts, but Jesus is primarily concerned with inner life—the condition of the heart. The law deals with what men do or do not do, but Jesus puts the emphasis upon what men are. The blessing of this is that when the heart is in right relationship with the Father, that person shall see God.

(7) "The peacemakers" (v. 9). Without doubt, there is a direct application here to those who do all within their power to settle disputes, thus making a semblance of peace. The fuller meaning, however, concerns those who share the good news of Christ, and thus reconcile men to God. Because Jesus was to repeatedly warn His followers of persecutions and troubles, He gave them encouragement about their new-found task.

(c) **The effects of true Christianity (vv. 13-16).** This teaching on *the blessed man* is often relegated to the kingdom of God and is looked upon as something entirely future, during the kingdom age. But this matter of "blessedness" is not entirely future. Genuine Christians exert a tremendous influence upon the world in which they live. To illustrate this, Jesus used two illustrations—object lessons as He was so apt to do. The first was that of salt which brings to our minds two of its functions. First, it enhances the flavor of food. So, we as Christians ought to enhance and improve all situations in which we are involved. Life to the Christian should be a glorious, thrilling adventure. Of course salt also makes men thirsty, and the Christian life, properly lived in a community, ought to make others want what we have. An organization which meets semiannually in our community has named itself "Win-Some Women," and really, every Christian ought to be a winsome person. In the second place, salt is a preservative. And Christians should exert a wholesome, preservative and protective influence upon society. Salt, if it is to be of value, must come into contact with another substance; that is, it should not be isolated. We as Christians dare not withdraw from the community, nor build walls of isolation around our own homes. We are to be a positive influence for good. Christians really should be the most respected citizens of the community; helpful neighbors and friends to all who live near them.

(d) **True righteousness identified (vv. 17-48).** The Lord

concludes this fifth chapter by setting forth the proposition of true righteousness, by saying, "Be ye therefore perfect, even as your Father which is in heaven is perfect." This is the ultimate—the goal toward which we move. Before He gave this assignment, He felt it necessary to do two things:

(1) The true significance of the law (vv. 17-20). Jesus must share with His hearers the true significance of the law. There are those who claim that He swept it aside, and it has no further value. However, He declares just the opposite. He had not come to destroy the law, nor even the works of the prophets who brought many additional traditions to the law. He taught that the law was of God, and although it was not complete revelation, it was given for a purpose. It was and is changeless, eternal, and inviolable. Not one little bit of it is to be classed as unimportant. The major problem was simply that it did not go far enough (v. 20). True righteousness must go far beyond the law. The Lord named the Pharisees, and we need to remember that they were the separationists of their day. They were very zealous about the services of the Temple; they carefully avoided contact with anything that they thought to be defiled. They chose their associates with great care; actually, they were holy in their own eyes, and they were proud of it.

(2) But Jesus said to them and to us, "But I say unto you"—that is, in contrast to their thinking and interpretation, we must go beyond what they have practiced. He substantiates His statement with several examples of what He has reference to in His assertion.

The law of murder: (vv. 21-26). We only call a man a murderer when he is actually proved guilty of killing someone else. The law judges only the outward act; God, however, is concerned with the very thoughts and motives that make for murder. What a man feels is important for it is followed by action. God reminds us that anger, contempt, hatred (v. 22) are such sins that they make worship impossible. In order to have a continuing right relationship with God, we must deal with these sins, and be reconciled to our fellow men. Opportunities of service and worship will then be open to us.

The law of adultery: (vv. 27-30). A man or woman is judged by mankind to have committed a serious sexual impurity, only when indulging in an illicit sexual act. However, Jesus goes to the heart of the matter and declares the lusting, the looking that leads up to the act, is likewise sinful and is a matter of the heart condition of an individual. Jesus concludes that harboring the desire is dangerous; that it would be better to take drastic measures necessary to avoid the act. In verses 29-30, He simply says that if a member of the body causes you to stumble, brings you into sin, get rid of it. He begins with the illustration of the eye. He is not commanding that we mutilate our bodies to get rid of sin, for this would not change the picture one iota. He chooses to picture two objects of the body—the eye, and the hand. These two objects speak of looking and doing. We ought to look away from temptation and move out of the area of doing.

Closely related to these sexual sins is the subject of divorce which is introduced at this place. The simplest way to solve the problem is *"Don't."* In very straightforward fashion, Jesus puts divorce and adultery in the same paragraph. He forbids it! God never intended man to enter into the marriage relationship in a light manner.

In the area of truthfulness (vv. 32-37), the law had forbidden perjury. But Jesus explained it with the deeper truth by saying that we should be so much a man of our word that we would not need to take an oath to convince people of our truthfulness.

Then there is the matter of revenge (vv. 38-42), and Jesus insists that we must "resist not evil." He is not saying to let evil take over. He is talking about indulging in personal revenge for wrongs done to us, even though it means personal loss in suffering or in property loss.

Finally, there is the illustration of the law of love. The law did not provide that man should hate his enemies, but Jewish tradition took it to mean that because it only insisted that man should love his neighbors and friends. Now, Jesus reminds us that even those who are not a part of the kingdom of God love these (5:46-47). We must go a step farther and love even our enemies—those unkind or unfriendly toward us.

In summation of the whole, Jesus simply said, "Be ye therefore perfect, even as your Father which is in heaven is perfect" (Matt. 5:48). Actually, we are to be mature in all of these things—purity, mercy, righteousness, in love—not only in keeping the law, but in doing that which the Spirit of the law would expect.

II. Our Relationship with God (Matt. 6)

Our generation is said to be the generation with the greatest number of frustrations and nervous breakdowns of any generation in history. There are more heart attacks than have ever been known because in a frantic effort to rise to the top, whether it be in the social world, in business, or the church, men are tearing themselves apart. But this chapter would center our attention on the best life—that is, the life that is centered on God, with a goal to please Him in all of life's activities.

There are two areas that Christ deals with in this chapter: (a) right motives and (b) right attitudes.

1. Right motives (6:1-18). In the first half of the chapter Jesus deals with our motives: What is it that causes us to act the way we do? Jesus asks that question in relation to three areas: namely, almsgiving, prayer, and fasting. Jesus never condemns any of these actions of life, but He does insist that the motive that causes us to act in any of these must be right.

Almsgiving may include all of our giving, whether to the church, or to the local scouting program, or to the United Fund. Giving to get your name in the paper or to get a plaque on the wall is a very low motive. Jesus says for this: "They have their reward." They receive the plaudits of the crowds, and it is done! Jesus advised that our giving ought to be a matter between the giver and God. Let us remember that God does see every act, including our giving, and when our motives are right in the giving, He will reward us accordingly. One word of caution. This does not forbid keeping careful records of your giving, or even of the officers of a church keeping records in order to complete reports for the general church and the governmental authorities.

Then Jesus turns His attention to prayer (vv. 5-15). Here again, certain of the Pharisees would purposely arrange to be at busy corners of the streets when the time of prayer arrived, and they would stand for long periods of time to impress those who passed by of the piety of their lives. Again, Jesus said they have their reward. Then He gave direction as to the prayer life. Remember, again, He is not condemning public prayer. This would be contrary to the teaching where He encouraged us to gather in groups to pray. He is only condemning prayers that are uttered to make a public impression on those who hear us. Prayer is a matter between man and his God, and hence, we pray best when we shut the world out, whether it be in the midst of a crowd, or in private. A full study of the prayer pattern which Jesus gives us here is well worthwhile and should be diligently studied.

The third area which Jesus calls attention to is fasting (6:16-18). Remember, again Jesus does not condemn it, but we are taught it should be done with real meaning and purpose.

2. Right attitudes (vv. 19-34). The latter half of this chapter deals with two sins which God's people ought to avoid. The first is that of piling up treasures and is often referred to as the "sin of the rich." However, it is possible that the poor are as guilty as the rich in their attitude toward riches. It is summed up in verse 24, where the Lord gives instruction that we cannot serve both the god of this world and the true God. The one thing that Jesus would have us remember is that this earth's treasures are fleeting. The other extreme of this is that of "worry" about tomorrow. Today is well taken care of, but where will I get enough to live tomorrow? This may not be an actual voiced expression, but it is so easily seen in many of our lives. Now remember again, this is not despising a man working for a living, or even the wise use of his assets. It does condemn our preoccupation with and worry about the making of a living. The secret of it all is found in verse 33—the secret of a happy, serene life!

III. Direction Concerning Needs—Encouragements and Warnings (Matt. 7)

This great lesson concludes with a series of teachings concerning certain needs of our lives.

1. Judgments (vv. 1-6). Because this verse begins with "Judge not," many take it away from the context and suggest we have no right to judge anyone about anything. This is contrary to the whole tenor of Scripture. Judgment is a God-given prerogative to be used carefully by mature people. In our daily lives we must constantly make judgments. The problem comes when we judge people for their motives, and hence, exercise a privilege that belongs to God alone. He sees the heart of a man. When we become harsh, cynical or critical, we can become faultfinders. All judgment ought to begin with ourselves (v. 3), and yet, all of us tend to excuse our sins as weaknesses and cover them up with this excuse or another. God does urge us (Gal. 6:1) to help a weaker brother, thus demanding good judgment, but only after we have gained a victory ourselves. Then of course comes judgment concerning our witness through the Word (v. 6).

2. Prayer (vv. 7-12). In commenting on this verse (7), often called the a-s-k of prayer, Macaulay suggests a definite progression in the words—"ask" which has to do with our needs in general; "seek" implies a desire to discover all new knowledge; "knock" suggests an effort to enter into a larger experience. The illustration comes from a normal experience of the family—a father and his son—with a final direction that because of your relationship to God, because of His liberality, because He gives good gifts to you, you ought to do the same for those who live around you. This has often been referred to as the "golden rule." Nothing wrong with the golden rule. It will not get a man to heaven, but every Christian should live up to the standard set by the golden rule.

3. Two roads, two gates (vv. 13-22). The picture here of the strait gate and the narrow way applies principally to salvation. Although there are many ways to come to Christ and His salvation, there is only one way to salvation, that is, in Christ. He is the strait gate, and He is the narrow road that leads to life. The picture may also be applied to the Christian life, for it has a price to be paid—we need to actively walk in the Christian way.

4. False teachers and their fruits (vv. 15-23). False teachers are active in every age of the world. We have them today, even as there were many of them in Christ's day. Jesus reminds us in verse 16, that the test of false teachers is in their fruits. This refers to both what they teach and to the lives they live.

5. Building and its results (vv. 24-27). The closing teaching of these three chapters is a natural, for Jesus had grown up in the carpenter's shop. Therefore, to talk about building must have been very real to Him.

All of us are building—either on God's truth or on some other foundation. Trouble and testing will come, for no one escapes sorrow, bereavement, and finally God's evaluation at either the Bema Seat of Christ, or the Great White Throne judgment. Then that which has not been built upon Christ will be swept away. Knowledge of God's Word will enable us to move in every area of life in the correct manner— determining what is right and wrong, true or false, and to make choices that will bear spiritual fruit.

6

Matthew 8:1–9:35

▰▰▰▰▰▰▰▰▰▰▰▰▰▰▰▰▰▰▰▰▰

The King Reveals His Power

THE CHAPTER OUTLINED:

INTRODUCTION
THE EXPOSITION
  I.   Power Over Disease (Matt. 8:1-17)
       1.   The Healing of the Leper (Matt. 8:1-4)
       2.   Healing of the Centurion's Servant (Matt. 8:5-13)
       3.   Healing of Peter's Mother-in-Law (Matt. 8:14-17)
 II.   Power Over Nature and Demons (Matt. 8:18-24)
       (a) The proposal of a scribe (v. 19)
III.   Power Over Sin (Matt. 9:1-17)
 IV.   Power Over Death (Matt. 9:18-25)

INTRODUCTION

As Jesus finished His teaching on the mount, His hearers were "astonished" (Matt. 7:28). He had spoken as "one having authority" (v. 29), in contrast to the teaching of the scribes. As He came down from the mountain the multitudes followed Him. In the lesson which He shared with them, the Sermon on the Mount (Matt. 5–7), Jesus had declared the principles of the kingdom. Now He is ready to give the proof of His power to banish from the earth the consequences of sin and to control even the elements of nature. In a series of ten miracles, recorded in these chapters, Matthew presents Jesus as the King of kings showing His power in many different areas of life.

THE EXPOSITION

The first miracles that Matthew records were in the area of physical healing. Disease has long been a concern of men everywhere, and it is one of the chief concerns of our own nation.

I. Power Over Disease (Matt. 8:1-17)

1. The Healing of the Leper (Matt. 8:1-4). It is interesting to note the first miracle Matthew chose, for we must remember that in the days of our Lord's sojourn upon the earth there were very strict laws concerning those afflicted with the dread disease of leprosy.

Whether or not this man was one who stood afar off and heard Jesus speak, or whether he had heard of Him from someone else, somehow this man had heard about Jesus and His power to heal. In contrast to the multitudes who merely followed Jesus, perhaps out of curiosity, the leper "worshipped him." His approach is extremely interesting, for he said, "Lord, if thou wilt." He apparently did not doubt the ability of Jesus to heal, but at this point, he was not sure as to whether He would be willing to do so. Jesus answered in a unique manner, by putting forth His hand and touching him

(v. 3). He did not hesitate to do that which the problem demanded, even though the ceremonial law forbade Him, or anyone else, to touch the unclean. He could have healed the leper with a single word from His lips, but He chose rather at this point to touch the man.

One has suggested that God never loves man at an arm's length, but extends His hand to touch him and make him whole. There is an application that ought to apply to every Christian—we cannot love people at a distance. We, too, must go into the various levels of life and different social stratas to reach men, for "all have sinned," whether in the high level of society, or in the low castes of a slum area. After the healing had taken place, the Lord gave the leper command that he should now comply with the ceremonial law and follow its requirements (8:4). Some have used this story to emphasize social concern, but we believe the story is included at this place to emphasize that until men come into a right relationship with God, through Jesus, no blessing will be complete. Heal the disease of leprosy (a picture of sin) and then do everything else that is necessary.

2. Healing of the Centurion's Servant (Matt. 8:5-13). Leaving the immediate area from which He had spoken the great Sermon on the Mount, and nearby where He had healed the leper, He came to Capernaum where He dealt with a different kind of physical need. It was here where he met a Roman Centurion who was a commander of the Roman Army, being over a group of 100 Roman soldiers. Historians tell us that the troops of the Roman Government were generally drawn, not from a distant land, but rather from the non-Jewish people living in the land of Palestine and surrounding countries. Although the man was a Roman commander, he had a compassion for his soldiers and servants, for we see him pleading not for himself but rather for a servant.

The disease is called "palsy" in verse 6, but in addition Matthew adds that he is "grievously tormented." This was a paralysis with contraction of the joints, and according to Dr.

Trench involves much suffering. And, when united, as it most often is in the hot climate of the East and of Africa, with tetanus, "grievously torments" and brings on dissolution rapidly. If the leper gives us a picture of sin, this victim of palsy gives us the picture of the results of sin—a crippling and helpless condition that requires a miracle!

Immediately Jesus offered to go to the centurion's home and heal the servant (v. 7), but the soldier knew that a Jew stepping into his house would be defiled, according to Jewish tradition. He also confessed his own unworthiness (v. 8) and used his own sphere of authority (vv. 8-9) to indicate something of the faith he had in Jesus Christ—in the realm of His supreme authority. He simply said to this effect: "I have an authority in the army whereby a command brings instant obedience; so, too, You have an authority, and a word from Your lips would cause the cure" (v. 8).

The response to the words of the centurion is interesting for it indicates something of the joy that it brought to the heart of the Lord. He spoke of a faith, the like of which he had not found in all of Israel (cf. v. 10). We live in the midst of a generation which says: "Show me, then I will believe." It is an easy thing to be a doubter! But before the centurion had any proof of a cure, he had the faith to believe that it would happen. Jesus responded by giving the centurion His word that His servant would be healed (v. 13).

Some perfectly natural questions might be asked—Does the degree or kind of faith matter? Are there degrees of faith? Would Jesus have healed this servant had the centurion's faith been weak? Notice what Jesus had to say about the subject of faith—particularly in Matthew 17:20.

3. Healing of Peter's Mother-in-Law (Matt. 8:14-17). In the corresponding passage written by Luke (4:38-39) we are given a few more details. He reminds us that this woman "was taken with a great fever." Many of us know something of the weakness that fever brings to the body and it was true in this case. They laid her upon her bed and then went to tell the

Lord of the sickness. There are a few practical truths here that we dare not pass: (a) Sickness comes to every home, whether it be Christian or not. (b) They told the Lord about the trouble, which ought to serve as a reminder that we, too, have access to Jesus; therefore, we have the privilege of bringing our loved ones, who are afflicted, to the Lord in prayer.

The Lord saw the woman and heard the petitions of His disciples, and He touched her. Matthew is explicit here by reminding us that He took her by the hand and lifted her up. The fever was gone. She rose and began immediately ministering to them—she attended to their needs. Again, the practical application: When we have been cured of the disease of sin, we are to give ourselves to God's service, to minister to Him in whatever manner He has planned for us. We ought to follow the example of Peter's mother-in-law and freely give of ourselves to His work.

Although three specific miracles are given to us here, it is not the end of the Lord's healing ministry, even in this chapter, for verses 16-17 tell of many other healing miracles. It is interesting to note that "when the even was come" they brought many others for healing. Why wait until evening? Mark tells us that it was the Sabbath (Mark 1:21, 19), and the Jewish law forbids leaving the home and bearing burdens. Many of these who came were carried there by their friends. Matthew reminds us that this was a fulfillment of the prophecy of Isaiah.

II. Power Over Nature and Demons (Matt. 8:18-24)

After this series of miracles of healing, Jesus announced to His followers His intention of leaving the area and going to the other side, presumably for a bit of relaxation from the busyness of life.

(a) **The proposal of a scribe (v. 19).** It would seem that this scribe had heard the Lord, as He taught; had watched Him perform miracles, and now was ready to follow Jesus, wherever He went (vv. 18-19). The desire of the scribe seemed to be perfectly in order and on the surface was totally sincere. However, the Lord did not encourage him in this desire. The Lord is able to look upon the heart, and without doubt, He saw more than we are able to see. Quickly He delineated the cost of true discipleship. Jesus reminded the scribe that to follow Him, a man must be willing to give up his home, his family, and move into an existence that may carry him afar (v. 20). Then another of His disciples wanted to go with the Lord, but he had immediate plans (v. 21). Most Bible scholars believe that he was simply asking a delay in his following, until his father had died. Jesus likewise refused this request, saying, "let the dead bury their dead."

A very practical way of saying this is that the Christian life has various priorities, but the Lord demands first place among all priorities.

With this teaching given, the Lord is now ready to continue His journey across the water, to the other side, and so Matthew records: "When he was entered into a ship, his disciples followed him." These disciples were committed to Him, and where He went, they went also. Suddenly they were overtaken by a violent storm. The waves rolled over the boat, and in the midst of their attempt to find rest, they were frightened by a storm. It did not waken the Lord, for Matthew reminds us that "he was asleep" (v. 24).

What a picture of life we have in this paragraph. As long as everything is running smoothly, men are satisfied to get along without God, but let trouble and disaster break around them and their morale is gone. Even Christians, who know the Lord and have His presence with them at all times, grow fearful when they do not see evidence of that presence in action. The disciples quickly awakened Him with what amounted to a prayer of fear: "Lord, save us: we perish." With a gentle reproval, the Lord responded: "Why are ye fearful, O ye of little faith?" The winds and the waves had brought fear not only to their hearts on account of the physical danger, but in a sense had robbed them of their faith to believe the Lord could or would keep them from danger. Have you been in some dangerous places recently? Have you lacked faith to believe that God is able to see you through? Would He say to you or to me, "O ye of little faith"?

Arriving at their destination, across the lake, in the country of the Gergesenes, they met two men under the control of demons. These men lived in the tombs and were so fierce that men did not dare to approach them—they did not even dare pass by that way. As Jesus approached, they cried out (actually, it was the voice of the demons crying out), "Art thou come hither to torment us before the time?" Satan and his host of demons know that there is a fixed time when they will be cast into the abyss, and they are not anxious to see the day approaching. They saw a way out—and pleaded that Jesus would permit them to go into the herd of swine. He gave the permission, and immediately the swine plunged head-long into the sea and were drowned (vv. 29-32). With the upsurge of the occult movement in our own generation, and the way in which men are turning to it, we cannot help but wonder how long it will be until we see something of a repetition of this kind of happening.

What were the results of that day in the life of Jesus? The people of the city heard what had happened to their swine, and they wanted no part of His ministry. They knew that He had driven the demons out of the men and that these two were made whole; but in contrast they had lost a herd of swine, and this was an expensive item, so they asked Jesus to leave the country. The practicalities are very evident for Jesus is in the business of saving men, and that becomes costly to some businesses, hence they want no part of it. They would rather see men suffer than lose a business venture.

III. Power Over Sin (Matt. 9:1-17)

Jesus returned back to Capernaum where He was known and welcomed. Upon His arrival, they brought a pitiable case to Him. The man they brought was paralyzed, quite helpless; apparently he had lost his speech and the ability to walk, for they carried him on a bed (or mat). The language would even suggest that this illness came upon the man as a result of his own sin. Let us again be reminded that sickness and sin are in the personal aspect, not necessarily tied together (cf. John 9:1-3), although palsy frequently came as a direct result of a life of sin. Jesus knowing all things, went to the heart of the problem by forgiving the man his sins. This forgiveness became the very thing for which the religious leaders who were present rebelled and called Jesus a blasphemer. Notice the order—healing came only after the announcement of "sins ·forgiven." He used the occasion as a proof of His own deity! They had not said it openly, but were talking it among themselves and believing it, that this statement, "Thy sins be forgiven thee," belonged only to God; and hence, Jesus was claiming to be God. They were right—Jesus had claimed it and would continue to claim it, but now in a very clear manner, He shows His authority and power tied into one package by forgiving the man his sins, and then publicly using His power to heal the man. The attitude of the multitude was that of praise and glory to God, but for the scribes there is no record of a change of heart. How differently people react to the actions of Jesus Christ.

Although Matthew does not mention much concerning his call to discipleship nor anything concerning the dinner he gave to the Lord, we discover from Mark and Luke that it was Matthew who gave the dinner which became the center of controversy. The fact that Jesus would eat with sinners caused the Pharisees to ask questions to which the Lord gave a ready answer. His answer in verse 12 should not be construed to mean that He was saying the Pharisees were "whole." That was their own estimation of their own worth, and Jesus was simply saying that if they were whole, they did not need a physician. Then the disciples of John took the occasion for the additional question as to fasting. The Lord did not criticize those who fasted. He, however, suggested that this was neither the time nor place for fasting for He was with them. It should have been a time of rejoicing. When He would leave them, there would be time for mourning and fasting. In addition, he reminded them that His new way of life was not a patched up garment but a new robe.

IV. Power Over Death (Matt. 9:18-25)

He has already shown His own authority and power over many diseases of both body and mind—over the forces of nature, and the demon world. Now, we are challenged with His power over the last enemy of men, even death itself.

Into the midst of the confrontation over the judgment of the Pharisees, a certain ruler came and worshiped Him, telling Him of the problem of death that had come into his own home (vv. 18-19). Now the Lord does not delay nor stay with the feasting. He left immediately to go to the home of the ruler, that He might minister. On the way to the ruler's house, yet another interruption takes place. A woman, suffering from a dread disease, had believed that if she could but "touch his garment, I shall be whole" (v. 21). She got through the crowds, and did just that—"touched the hem of his garment," and was healed instantly and completely (v. 22). And then, He arrived at the home of the ruler, and His first action was to dismiss the mourners who had come to assist in the burial. All of the language here, and in Luke's account, seems to demand our understanding that the "girl was dead"—that is, her spirit had left the body. When He announced that she was asleep, the crowd laughed Him to scorn. But how tenderly He deals with the girl. He went into her room, took her by the hand and commanded her to arise. The girl obeyed, and Matthew simply records that this brought fame to Him in all of the land.

Matthew concludes this section by citing two additional miracles. The total of all of these miracles brought additional hatred to the hearts of His enemies. In an attempt to ɔlain the numerous miracles, they simply declared He was a tool of Satan, using the power which Satan was giving Him even to cast out demons (v. 34).

So, in the present hour, the power of Christ and His Gospel divides men into two camps—those who believe and gain the victory; the others who refuse to believe, and who grow more and more vicious in the attacks they make upon him.

7

Matthew 9:35–12:50

Expanded Witness – Widening Gulf

THE CHAPTER OUTLINED:

INTRODUCTION
THE EXPOSITION
I. An Expanding Witness (Matt. 9:36–10:42)
   1. The Background (Matt. 9:36-38)
   2. The Called Apostles (10:1-4)
   3. The Commission to the Twelve (10:5-15)
   4. A Caution to the Twelve (10:16-23)
   5. Encouragement for the Twelve (10:24-42)
   6. Demonstration Given for the Sake of John (11:2-19)
   7. Christ Speaks as Judge (vv. 20-27)
II. A Widening Gulf (Matt. 12:1-50)
   1. The Question Concerning the Sabbath (12:1-21)
   2. The Great Principle Involved (vv. 6-8)

INTRODUCTION

In this section of Matthew's account we discover a variety of incidents beginning with the introduction of the apostles and their commissioning. As the story unfolds, Matthew points out some of the perils encountered and gives a warning as to the high cost of being a disciple. There is the question that came to the Lord from John the Baptist through some of John's disciples, and then a public commendation of John by Jesus. Next comes a condemnation for some of the cities where He had preached and been rejected. Certain incidents are noted in which Jesus enters into sharp conflict with the Pharisees over Sabbath observance. Toward the end of the section, the Lord cast out demons, and the Pharisees once again charged Him with being in league with Satan. The section closes in a very personal way, in which the relationship of the Son and His mother and brethren is used as a picture of a new relationship He is establishing with all who will be His disciples (cf. 12:50).

THE EXPOSITION

As we move into the exposition of this lengthy portion, keep in mind that it is not the intent to carefully study every section in a word-for-word study. But rather, we desire to discover the movement of the life of Christ as He enlists and commissions His helpers, sends them once more to the people of Israel, and then as we see Him approaching the end of His personal teaching ministry and moves toward the cross.

I. An Expanding Witness (Matt. 9:36—10:42)

1. The Background (Matt. 9:36-38). Wherever the Lord Jesus went, we discover great multitudes following Him. Without doubt there were various reasons for this following, but the fact is that they followed Him. As He saw them, His heart was moved with compassion, and He tells us why—"they fainted," literally were tired and lay down. It is another way of saying what men are saying today—they were frustrated, did not know where to turn. He also tells us that they were "scattered abroad, as sheep having no shepherd." It is the same answer as we hear today—"no one cares." But they were wrong then, for the heart of Jesus was "moved with compassion"—moved with a heart of love that was great enough to do something about their condition. He shared His heartthrob with His disciples in other words that are equally fitting for today: "The harvest truly is plenteous, but the labourers are few." We know that when a harvest is ready it must be reaped immediately or it will be lost. Winds and rain will destroy the abundant harvest in the field; and so, too, there are many enemies who would destroy the harvest of souls to which the Lord here makes reference. On the other hand, "the labourers are few." Of all those who should be responding to the call for laborers, only a few of God's people respond to the challenge to do the work of the Lord.

It is with this background that Jesus gave a word to the disciples which is still effective today: "Pray ye therefore the Lord of the harvest, that he will send forth labourers into his harvest" (Matt. 9:38). We can do nothing else until first we have prayed for laborers. God's part is to send forth those laborers who will do His work. We can know before it happens, that when we are faithful in praying for laborers, God will be faithful in answering our prayers and sending forth those laborers.

2. The Called Apostles (10:1-4). It is interesting to note that He did tell His disciples to pray (9:38), and now in chapter 10, verse 1, when He had called "unto him his twelve disciples, he gave them power." I quote a missionary who said: "to pray for laborers is very dangerous, for God may ask you to go in response to your prayers." God expects us to put feet under our prayers—if our prayers require feet. It is important to pray, even as He suggested, but it is also important to respond to His call when He makes that call to us personally.

In the listing of the apostles, it is always Peter who is

named first, while Judas Iscariot is named last. Matthew in this record is the only one who refers to himself as "the publican," while later on Thomas by his actions and words became known as "Thomas the doubter." Note in verse 1 that He called each of these twelve men and gave them all the same power—against unclean spirits, to cast them out; to heal all manner of sickness and all manner of disease. God still does the calling of men to do service for Him. Sometimes men choose to become leaders in the fields of Christian service, but unless God has called, they walk on very dangerous ground. He always empowers those He calls and commissions to go forth in service for Him. Although each of these came from varying backgrounds and each had his own strengths and weaknesses, the Lord empowered all. Remember, in making application to present-day service, He likewise promised to empower His workers in our generation (28:18-20) . . . "All power is given unto me. . . . Go ye therefore . . . and, lo, I am with you alway." He goes with us, because He dwells within us.

3. The Commission to the Twelve (10:5-15). This brief paragraph was given as an immediate commission and should not be construed to be permanent. When Christ gave the commission to the church, He commanded to "Go ye into all the world"; but here, it was a message to be carried to "the lost sheep of the house of Israel" (v. 6). Their preaching was to be the exact message of both John the Baptist (3:2), and that of Jesus (4:17), namely, "the kingdom of heaven is at hand." He commissioned them to do as He had been doing, that is, to "heal the sick, cleanse the lepers, raise the dead" (v. 8). Verses 10-11 seem to lay stress upon two words, "provide not"—don't take time to get material things—there is much work to be done, and not much time in which to do that work. The emphasis is upon the urgency of the task, not upon material gain. The other side of the story is found in the latter part of verse 10 where He also taught that the workman was worthy of his food. Those who give their lives in the service of the Lord are still compelled to pay their bills. However, God does provide for them, largely through His people—those who benefit by the ministry of the men God calls to do service for Him. Remember, these were directions being given for those who were to go into strange towns to preach—this was not a permanent pastorate, but a continuing one in many cities and villages. In verse 11 Jesus gave direction concerning this—they were to seek out the worthy houses and accept the hospitality of these homes. Verse 14 would suggest that sometimes they would not be received; and when they were rejected, they were to shake off the dust from their feet and depart. When they were well received, they were to leave blessing and peace in the home; when they were rejected, they were to withdraw their blessing and leave.

4. A Caution to the Twelve (10:16-23). To further fortify the disciples as He sent them forth, the Lord issued a word of caution lest they believe that everyone would receive them gladly. He had already commissioned them to go to the "lost sheep of the house of Israel," and now He uses a picture in which the disciples themselves are pictured as the sheep, and He is sending them forth in the midst of wolves. Therefore, they should be very wise, yet harmless. Jesus predicted that the disciples would suffer because they dared to speak for Him. The hatred against the Lord was already beginning to show, and He promised His disciples that they would not be free from the same kind of a hatred (cf. vv. 18, 22, 24-25). Some would try to hold this hatred to only the day of the disciples, but things have not actually changed very much. They will still hate you for taking a stand for Christ. Perhaps not as openly today in our own nation, but it is becoming increasingly so even here. Then Jesus reminded them that they would be brought before councils, and synagogues, governors and kings (vv. 17-18, 21), which finally includes even the family ties that are so very close. As a matter of fact, perhaps the most difficult of all opposition is that which arises within the family circle, for here, you would expect acceptance.

In the fact of all this opposition, which the Lord told his disciples would be their lot, He promises them three things. The first promise was the help of the Spirit who dwells within (vv. 19-20). In the time of trial, they would not need to worry about what they ought to say, for the Spirit indwelt them and would speak through them. We ought not to assume that the Spirit of God will supply our need for proper words if we fail to prepare for a lecture or a sermon. This has often been done, but it is wrong. The issue here is that when in the midst of trial, Christ will give wisdom and courage to speak out for Him (cf. v. 18).

The second promise is that of total victory. There is coming a total victory for the people of God after much persecution, and He promises the one "that endureth to the end shall be saved" (v. 22). Some have taken this as a demand on the part of the Lord for the Christian to endure persecution as a way of gaining salvation—but such would deny the truth of God's grace. We are saved by that which He has accomplished. Dr. A. C. Gaebelein has given what I believe to be the best commentary on this section, and really the only satisfactory answer to the problem. Picking up a paragraph from him concerning the persecution, he says:

> The most bitter persecution is now promised them (the disciples) by our Lord (vv. 21-22). These words are perhaps the most important in the whole chapter. They are a kind of a key to the entire chapter. The giving of the testimony by Jewish disciples concerning the kingdom of the heavens is according to the words of our Lord to continue till He comes again. The testimony which was begun by the apostles up to the time when Israel rejected once more the offers of mercy from the risen Lord, when He was still waiting for their repentance as a nation, is an unfinished testimony. After that offer was again rejected, the great parenthesis, the Church Age, began, and during this age, there is no more testimony of the kingdom of heavens. When the church is complete, and the rapture has taken place, then the Lord begins to deal with His people Israel again . . . then Jewish believers will once again take up the testimony of "The Kingdom of the heavens

is at hand." Then, during the tribulation (never now) it will mean enduring to the end and salvation will come, then by the visible return of the Son of Man from heaven.

The third promise is that Christ will come again (v. 23). To us, this means that we shall not have finished preaching the Gospel to the Jews, when our Lord comes back and takes us to be with Him. Our task as witnesses will not be completed when He comes again, and it will then divert to a different kind of witness during the tribulation period. Once again the emphasis will be upon the witness to the Jewish nation.

5. Encouragement for the Twelve (10:24-42). Jesus concludes His direction to the twelve by giving them some real words of encouragement. Dr. Jacobson, in commenting on these verses, points out that the section contains eight important principles for those who are doing God's work:

(a) We are not to expect preferential treatment at the hands of the world (vv. 25-26). (b) We are to proclaim the Lord's message (vv. 26-27). (c) We are to have a healthy respect for God (v. 28). (d) We may count on God's personal concern (vv. 29-31). (e) We must confess our Lord openly (vv. 32-33). (f) We must put Christ in first place in our lives (v. 34). (g) We must lose ourselves in our Lord's service (vv. 38-39). (h) We are to receive Christ's workers as we would receive Christ himself (v. 40).

The instruction closes, and Matthew does not choose at this point to tell us anything more concerning the twelve whom Jesus had sent forth. Matthew continues the story—for remember He is presenting the story of Christ the King of the Jews, by simply stating that Jesus departed thence to teach and preach in their cities.

6. Demonstration Given for the Sake of John (11:2-19). John the Baptist was in prison, and sent two of his followers to talk with Jesus. They asked a question very bluntly, "Art thou he that should come, or do we look for another?" Don't criticize John too harshly, for remember he is in jail, and until you have championed the cause of Jesus Christ and been placed in jail because of your testimony, it is difficult to understand. He had been given a sign and understood fully the fact that Jesus was the Messiah (John 1:29-34). He had declared Him to be just this, but now there is the question— "Why does He permit this to come to me?" Jesus was very compassionate toward John, and verse 4 tells us that He sent the two back to John with this word: "Go, and shew John again those things which ye do hear and see." Luke in his record of this same event says that "in that same hour" Jesus performed many cures. Apparently these were done at this time in order to give John's disciples a demonstration of His continuing power to fulfill His ministry. Jesus included a special word of commendation concerning John that must have brought real blessing to those who carried it back to him: "Among them that are born of women there hath not risen a greater than John the Baptist: notwithstanding he that is least in the kingdom of heaven is greater than he" (Matt. 11:11). Jesus called John the greatest of the great men in history up to this moment. Let us remember that John lived at the close of the Old Testament days and at the time of the coming of the Messiah. He was the very one who had the privilege of knowing, through revelation, that Jesus was the "Son of God." He had the privilege of presenting Him as the One who had come to take "away the sin of the world." However, Jesus went on to say to the twelve, and to us through them, "notwithstanding he that is least in the kingdom of heaven is greater than he" (v. 11). John knew Jesus in the flesh, but every Christian from that day until now has the risen Christ abiding within. It might be said concerning every one who names the name of Christ, that we have a greater privilege than John ever had; but the tragedy is most of us live far beneath our privileges.

Verse 12 is often called a difficult passage and one with many interpretations. However, I am inclined to take the position of Dr. Gaebelein, who says:

> The violent who take the kingdom by violence are not unsaved
> sinners, who seek salvation and that salvation must be taken by

force. Salvation is by grace, it is God's free gift, and the sinner is not saved through and in his violent efforts, but in believing in the Lord Jesus Christ. The Pharisees and scribes who stand here before our Lord are the violent who take the Kingdom of the Heavens (never the Gospel) by force and seize on it. Our Lord says "from the days of John the Baptist until now." The forerunner, John, was violently rejected by the Pharisees. This foreshadowed the rejection of the King, the rejection of the preaching of the kingdom, and the kingdom itself. In this seizing upon the kingdom, rejecting it, the Kingdom of the Heavens suffered violence.

In the paragraph which follows Jesus asks a very pertinent question, then proceeds to give answer to it. "But to whom shall I liken this generation?" (v. 16). The answer is very enlightening—"It is like unto children sitting in the markets, and calling unto their fellows [companions]." One brief word could sum it up—*"complainers."* John had come, he had not been a part of their game of eating and drinking, and they said, "he hath a demon." Then Jesus came, and the same crowd accused Him of eating and wine drinking, and of being a friend of tax-gatherers and of sinners. John was too strict, and they were dissatisfied with him. The Lord came. He showed mercy to the sinners, the outcasts, even healed the lepers, and they accused Him of eating and drinking. They put Him on the level of the wine-drinking crowd of the community. It is simply the picture of man, who in his natural state is never happy with God's methods and ways (cf. Rom. 8:7). Then beginning with verse 20, the Lord gives a preview of His role as judge upon a throne.

7. **Christ Speaks as Judge (vv. 20-27).** "Then began he," that simply says this is something new. He had not done this before. The cities which He mentions had been greatly privileged. Works of power, works which showed some of the very power of God, had been shown in their midst, yet they repented now. He reminds them that Tyre and Sidon had not had the same privilege. The responsibility of Chorazin and Bethsaida is therefore greater than the responsibility of the

cities of Tyre and Sidon.

A very practical application in the area of judgment seems to be here; that is, the measure of relationship is always the measure of responsibility. It would be very applicable to remind us that the dark nations of the world, into which the Gospel has not gone, have less responsibility than does our own nation. In like manner, those of us who have the "whole Bible" are the more responsible to share it, both by lip and by life, with those who do not have it. Jesus likewise reminded them that even though some of these cities had been destroyed physically, there was yet a further judgment awaiting them—"in the day of judgment" (v. 24). This life does not end all of the suffering and punishment for sin to those who refuse to accept the "way God has provided" as the escape from the punishment for sin.

Jesus closes the paragraph with a brief prayer, speaking to the Father thanking Him for hiding this truth from "the wise and prudent." He is simply inferring that these people, through intellectual pride, rule out as untrue anything which they cannot understand. Jesus never puts a premium on ignorance, nor does He hold His gift of understanding to the world's so-called intellectuals. He reveals truth to whom He will reveal it, because He is God. The way He did things was good in His sight, and that is all that is essential. Jesus finished this message by simply stating once again that the Father, as the great giver of all good things, has delivered to Him, the Son, all things. Now, as the Saviour of the world, He is ready to give good things to all who will come to Him (vv. 28-30). This is a gracious invitation to all who are under the weight of unforgiven sins and also to those whose sins are forgiven, but who have not found rest in Him. We are to come to Him—we are to take His yoke—that is, enter into fellowship with Him.

II. A Widening Gulf (Matt. 12:1-50)

This chapter brings into focus the hatred of Israel against

the Lord and His rejection by His own. It is the turning point in this gospel record of the offer by Jesus to be king of His people; and with the rejection of this offer, there is also the postponement of the kingdom.

1. The Question Concerning the Sabbath (12:1-21). It arose out of the fact that Jesus and His disciples walked through a field of grain on "the sabbath day." Remember, it is a very sacred day to the Jews—the seventh day of the week. Dr. C. I. Scofield has some very excellent notes on "the sabbath day" at 12:1. Without doubt, as they walked through the field, they were hungry, and simply began to pick the ears of corn. It is not a matter of walking out of the way to do it, but rather of walking through the field. The Pharisees saw it, for they were watching for places to find fault with Jesus. They immediately called it to His attention, and He defended the right of His disciples to satisfy their hunger.

Jesus answered the Pharisees and their criticism, by referring to David (v. 3), and to the priests (v. 5). The argument was simply that if David and his followers could break a ceremonial law in its form, while keeping it in spirit; it must be right to so interpret the Sabbath law. Then there was the illustration of the priests, who served in the Temple on the Sabbath. Again the argument is that a literal cessation of manual labor, without any exception whatever the reason, was never intended by the Lord when He gave the law concerning the Sabbath.

2. The Great Principle Involved (vv. 6-8). Jesus now claims to be greater than the Temple, because He is the One for whom the Temple was erected; and He is the temple in which the very God of gods dwells. Likewise, He is the Lord of the Sabbath. In other words, Jesus told them that if they only understood the principle that all forms of worship are to help men, that the Sabbath was made for man, and not man for the Sabbath; they would have solved their own problems.

The violent hatred of men toward the Saviour continues throughout the chapter, whether He heals (as He does) the man with the withered hand (vv. 10-24); or casts out demons (vv. 22-29). It was this latter instance at verse 24 that actually brought about the crisis. The Lord closed His argument at verse 30 by saying that in the conflict men must choose sides. Man cannot remain neutral.

Verses 31-32 describe the sin "that shall not be forgiven"—often referred to as the "unpardonable sin"—that is, refusing to accept the evidence of the Holy Spirit and His working cannot be forgiven.

Verse 50 is the climax of it all: "For whosoever shall do the will of my Father." This is of utmost importance. His will is that we might all give Jesus Christ the place of Lordship in our lives as well as our words. This leads to an increasing service with Christ as we share in a great family relationship.

8

Matthew 13:1-53

━━━━━━━━━━━━━━━━━━━━━━━━━━━━━━━━

The Mysteries of the Kingdom of Heaven

THE CHAPTER OUTLINED:

INTRODUCTION
THE EXPOSITION
TEACHING THE MULTITUDES
    1. The Parable of the Sower and the Seed (vv. 3-23)
       The Explanation of the Parable (vv. 19-23)
    2. The Parable of the Wheat and the Tares (13:24-30; 36-43)
    3. The Parable of the Grain of Mustard Seed (vv. 31-32)
    4. The Parable of the Leaven (13:33)
    5. The Parable of the Hid Treasure (13:44)
    6. The Pearl of Great Price (13:45-46)
    7. The Parable of the Dragnet (13:47-50)
CONCLUSION

INTRODUCTION

The thirteenth chapter of Matthew is very important to all who would fully understand the life and teachings of the Lord while He dwelt upon the earth. In Matthew 12 we discovered a breach between the Lord and the religious leaders of His day. Now Jesus is approaching a continuing effort on their part to rid themselves of the One who had, by both word and act, declared himself to be the Son of God, the promised Messiah, the King of the Jews. The time had come when it was essential for Him to reveal some things that would happen during the time He would be gone from them, and the direction in which the world would move during His absence. In light of this, He gave them this teaching by means of parables.

The great mass of people continue to build their optimistic hopes for the enlargement of the church and a growing good works among men through a gross misinterpretation of the teaching which Jesus gave in this chapter. There need be no question about the reason for the method which He chose, for He tells us plainly. In verse 11 is the answer: "Because it is given unto you to know the mysteries of the kingdom of heaven, but to them it is not given." Then verses 34-35: "All these things spake Jesus unto the multitude in parables; and without a parable spake he not unto them: That it might be fulfilled which was spoken by the prophet, saying, I will open my mouth in parables; I will utter things which have been kept secret from the foundation of the world." This chapter then deals with the mysteries concerning the kingdom.

THE EXPOSITION

This discourse involving seven parables involves three distinct movements on the part of the Lord. The first of these was spoken by the seaside and to a multitude of people (vv. 1-35). Then He left the multitudes "and went into the house," where He continued His teaching, but this time only to His disciples (vv. 36-50). Finally, he addresses His disciples with a question, giving instruction concerning their responsibility during the age immediately ahead (vv. 51-53).

TEACHING THE MULTITUDES

Matthew begins by establishing the time of the discourse—"The same day." This has been called, by some, our Lord's busy day because so much is recorded of it. There are those who suggest that the crowd was so great that no home would accommodate them, hence they moved to the out-of-doors. Obviously, interest was very keen and enthusiasm for the teaching of Jesus was on the increase. The multitudes were interested in hearing this great Teacher who had come up from the multitudes. However, there must be more to the story than simply the large crowds. It was when the leaders in Israel had begun their rejection of Him, and after He had clearly announced a "new thing" (cf. Matt. 12:49-50). He is now turning to the Gentile nations, and so this passage tells us He "sat by the seaside" (cf. Rev. 17:15). The withdrawal of Jesus to a place by the seaside to teach may be taken as a dispensational foreshadowing of the national setting aside of Israel a bit later, and the preaching of the Gospel among the Gentiles. The seven parables, which Jesus is about to teach, give us the mysteries of the kingdom while the King himself is in rejection and absent from the earth. It is during this time that the church is being gathered out from among the nations. When that "body" is completed, the Lord will come for it, receive it unto himself, and then later return to the earth again with the church, set up His kingdom, restore Israel, and with His saints reign over all the world.

Matthew further suggests that this message was heard by "great multitudes." They loved to hear the Lord Jesus teach and preach. It was the unbelieving religious leaders who were against Him. Why did He attract such great crowds? There was spiritual light, power and blessings in the messages He taught, and this attracted the crowds. Someone has suggested that "He never held a great pulpit, but He reached the crowds."

He went into a ship—perhaps used that as His pulpit—and began to teach. This time Matthew records, "And he spake many things unto them in parables" (v. 3). A parable in its original meaning suggests "a placing beside," "a comparison." One has defined a parable as an earthly story with a heavenly meaning. By teaching in parables, our Lord emphasized and explained a spiritual teaching by comparing it with something well known by His hearers. Thomas Taylor said: "Our Saviour borroweth His comparisons from easy and familiar things, such as the sower, the seed, the ground, the growth, the withering, the answering or failing of the sower's expectations, all things well known and by all these would teach us some spiritual instruction, for there is no earthly thing which is not fitted to put us in mind of some things heavenly." As you think about the number of things Christ used from which to draw examples, you will be amazed at His methods of teaching truths. Just a few of them come to mind—the sun, the wind, fire and water, a mother hen gathering her chicks, a coin, the wedding garments and feast, children asking their father for a bit of bread—and with all of these, the application of spiritual truth.

1. The Parable of the Sower and the Seed (vv. 3-23). This first parable is one of the two which the Lord explained. We look first at the parable, then at the interpretation, followed by the teaching which He would have us gain from it.

The implication of the parable is that the sower did not sow in a garden at his own home; but rather, he went forth into open country where a path crosses through the cultivated land. There were thorns growing there and rocks dotted the surface of the landscape. There were some patches that were hard, and others that were extremely fertile. It is not hard to identify the sower as the Lord Jesus, for He was the original sower of the Word. Nor is it hard to identify the seed, for in explaining this parable, He said: "But he that received seed into the good ground is he that heareth the word" (v. 23).

It would be expected that with Jesus doing the sowing and with the seed—the Word of God—doing the work for which it was intended, it would grow up in every place bearing precious fruit. But He reminds us that such is not the case.

In the present age no man can ever tell what the sowing of the Word will accomplish. Its success or failure is a mystery to us and it seems to depend upon the character of the soil upon which it falls. (1) In the parable some of the seed fell by the wayside. The soil may have been good and capable of bearing a harvest, but the trouble lay in the fact that it had become so hardened that the seed, instead of falling into it, fell only upon the hard surface where the birds could easily find it and devour it. (2) Some seed fell on ground nearby that was rocky. The topsoil was good, but there was not enough of it. The seed fell into the soil and got a start. It looked very promising for a little while, but there was nothing to nourish it. The bright prospects soon came to an end, for when the hot rays of the sun fell upon the young growth it "withered away." (3) Still another portion of the seed fell among thorns. Here again, it would seem that the soil was good, for it furnished nourishment for the thorns. But the thorns were in the ground first and used up all the fertility of the ground. (4) Finally, there was also some seed that fell on good ground. The soil was in good condition to receive the seed and to give it a real opportunity to grow and bring forth a harvest. Here, although there was a variation in the amount, according to verse 8, all of it bore fruit. Then as Jesus closed the parable, He gave a very solemn appeal (v. 9). We often place emphasis upon the responsibility of Christians to share the Gospel with those who have not received it. But here, the Lord speaks with equal emphasis upon the responsibility of men to hear. Every person has ears, and hence, power to receive. God will hold every man responsible to attend to the preaching of the Word of God as it goes forth from the lips of teachers and preachers of the Word.

The parable brought an immediate response from the disciples, "Why speakest thou unto them in parables?" (v. 10). They had not heard a parable from His lips before. He had always spoken in simple words, easily to be understood by every one, and now for the first time He spoke, and they could not comprehend. It was a veiled statement. Jesus gave them His answer, and we ought to hear it clearly! "Because it is given unto you to know the mysteries of the kingdom of heaven, but to them it is not given" (v. 11). The disciples had received the Lord and the truth He had given them, but Israel had rejected Him; therefore, what they had would be taken away from them. Here is a spiritual truth that needs to be emphasized today in the church.

The true believers have, and will continue to have, understanding of His truth; while the apostate church—those who have heard but have rejected the truth—will lose even that which she boasts to have. In answering the disciples, Jesus quoted a passage from Isaiah 6:9-10, and He declares that this prophecy in Isaiah is fulfilled in them. He thus indicates that the reason they do not understand is due to the lack of willingness to receive it in time past. The Jews of Jesus' day had actually closed their eyes and ears to what they could have known. To people who turn away from so much truth as they had heard, God will not give a fuller revelation of knowledge. The parables of this chapter are actually a revelation of God's purpose for the world between the death of Christ and His coming again. Now, Jesus declares the disciples to be "blessed," because they are *seeing and hearing* these things. The prophets foretold the coming of Messiah; they even predicted His suffering and death, as for example Isaiah 53, but it is evident they did not understand how all of it could be fulfilled in one person.

The Explanation of the Parable (vv. 19-23). The individual who hears the Word of the kingdom but does not understand it will find that the wicked one comes and catches away what was sown in his heart. This is the one that received seed by the wayside. This group Jesus said does not understand the

Word. But it is not a question of intellectual understanding, for the Lord says that the Word was sown in the heart. It could have been accepted or rejected, but the heart would not have the truth—would not receive it. No sooner does the seed fall on this hard ground, than the wicked one comes, even as do the birds of the air, and devours the seed. The birds represent the wicked one. He is always ready, with his assistants, to twist and cause men to reject the Word of God. Let it be noticed that birds are again mentioned in the parables (the third), and there again, the birds represent evil.

The Word that falls on the rocky places is the seed that is received with joy, yet has no root in the soil of the heart, hence it is for a short time only. Then when trials and difficulties come, this type is immediately offended (vv. 20-21).

The third group, represented in verse 22, is easily understood and hardly needs comment, yet it is so essential in our generation. The world, the pleasures of this world, the deceitfulness of riches, seems to hold the spotlight everywhere today. The things of God become choked out even as thorns choke out the seed sown into the ground.

Finally, comes the seed down upon the good ground (v. 23) which produces the harvest in varying quantity. The soil was in a condition to receive the seed, for there was no hardened path here, no stony subsoil, and no thorns. The seed was the same in all of the ground, and even in this good ground, yet the ratio of the yield is different. Perhaps it is sufficient for us to observe here that even among true Christians there will be a difference in the fruitfulness of their lives, possibly depending on the degree of their yieldedness to Christ.

2. The Parable of the Wheat and the Tares (13:24-30; 36-43). This second parable is the last which Jesus explained to His disciples. Again, note that the explanation is given in response to the request of the disciples. The very form of the request gives us the emphasis Jesus had placed upon the matter of the tares. There is a brief statement concerning the

sower that emphasizes his sowing was in "his" field. The enemy came into the field, which did not belong to him, and likewise sowed seed, which the Lord identified as "tares." The tares are generally identified with a weed called "darnell," which in the early stages of growth looks so much like wheat that it escapes detection. Only when the plants mature can the difference between them be plainly seen. In the parable it was "when the blade was sprung up, and brought forth fruit" that the tares appeared. It was clear to the servants that the tares did not spring up of themselves (v. 27); hence the question of verse 28. The answer the Lord gives is that it came as a result of the enemy who had sown the tares in the field. The first thought of the servants was that of going into the field and pulling out the tares. The Lord gave other direction—"Let both grow together"—wait until harvest time, and then the tares can be gathered up first and made ready to burn, while the wheat will be harvested. His direction is very natural; for the sake of the good, let the two grow together, lest with destroying the bad, the good will also suffer. We ought also to call attention to the fact that the enemy worked during the night; which is always the time for "dirty work" at the hands of an enemy of man.

Before interpreting this second parable, the Lord spoke two other parables, which we look at briefly.

3. The Parable of the Grain of Mustard Seed (vv. 31-32).

To this parable, Jesus gave no direct interpretation, so it is essential that we interpret very carefully. The mustard seed, Jesus tells us, is "the least of all seeds." But this one, when it is sown, grows up and becomes greater than all herbs, becoming "a tree." The mustard seed ordinarily grows up to be a garden shrub and never has branches large enough to hold birds, or even give shade enough for the birds. But in this case, we have a shrub coming from the mustard seed that becomes a tree—thus outdoing itself. It became something that it was never intended to become. Just so, with the Church of Jesus Christ, that is the present-day, professing church, which has become something that Jesus never intended it should become. The kingdom started small, but in the world it grew very large. Today the church, instead of being separate from the world, has reached the stage that it mingles with the world and actually helps to dictate its policies. Then the second thing we need to note is that the birds came to lodge in the branches of this "shrub"—tree. Remember, in the first parable, Jesus said the seed that fell by the wayside was devoured by the fowls and Jesus identified the "fowls" with "the wicked one." The interpretation follows that the birds that lodge in the branches of the mustard tree are those under the direction of Satan. He, through his followers, sits in the important places of the professing church and dictates the policies of that portion of the church, elects its officers, and officiates at its world conclaves. We need to make the sharp distinction between the professing church and the true possessing church of Jesus Christ.

4. The Parable of the Leaven (13:33). This parable is another very short one—only one verse is recorded. There are those who teach that the leaven is the Gospel, introduced into the world by the church, and having a continuing influence upon the life of the world for good, until finally its effects will be total world good.

We do not believe this to be the interpretation, because in every other place in the Scripture where leaven is used it is the symbol or type of evil. The entire thrust of this series of parables is that there will be a mixture of good and evil from beginning to the end. In the first parable, three quarters of the seed sown is inoperative. In the second, there is the sowing of the good seed, then the sowing of the tares, and Jesus commanded that there be no separation until the end of the age. In the sowing of the mustard seed, there is a seed developing into that which was never intended. To interpret leaven in this place as something good is contrary to each of the other parables in this group.

Dr. C. I. Scofield has an excellent paragraph in his footnotes concerning leaven, which will help clarify this point. Accepting then the fact that leaven is error, evil, corruption, notice that it is placed into "three measures of meal." The meal stands for truth, for Christ and His Word. The leaven corrupts the meal. It changes that which is good by attacking in a hidden way its purity till it has pervaded the whole mass. The Lord is simply teaching how evil doctrine will corrupt the fine meal, the truth of the Word. It will continue to work in professing Christendom; yet, will not totally pervade all, for the true believers are still in the world, and they are the hindering force to the full leavening process of evil. (Dr. G. Campbell Morgan, *The Gospel According to Matthew*, or A. C. Gaebelein, *The Gospel of Matthew*, give additional help in this section.)

5. The Parable of the Hidden Treasure (13:44). After Jesus had dismissed the crowds, He went into the house, and here, in answer to the request of the disciples, He explained the second parable. We have looked at His interpretation, so proceed with the balance of instruction He gives to His disciples. This fifth one speaks of a "treasure hid in a field." We believe that Israel is the treasure in the field (cf. Exod. 19:5). When the Lord came from heaven He found His people in the field. Israel was already related to God through His covenant; and when Christ died upon the cross, He purchased the whole world, including the people who are His earthly treasure. However, he did not take possession of the treasure, but it is still hidden in the field which He bought with so great a price. During this age the treasure is kept hidden in the world; but at His return, He will lift the treasure, they will claim Him as their Messiah, and Israel will be saved. An excellent comment on this passage is found in Romans 11:25 and following.

6. The Pearl of Great Price (13:45-46). The second object which the Lord obtained by His work of redemption is "one pearl of great price," and is only fulfilled by His true church. The study of the formation of the pearl is an interesting one, and there are many precious truths to be gained from such a study. It is a beautiful picture of the way in which the church is being formed during this age. Though it is composed of many numbers, known only to Him, it is still being formed. However, the day will come when He will take the church unto himself into the air, and thus be with his "Bride" through all eternity. When He comes to take possession of Israel, the treasure hid in the field, His church will be with Him.

7. The Parable of the Dragnet (13:47-50). This parable falls into the completion of the age in which we live. At the end of this age, there will be good and bad in the professing kingdom. The dragnet is let down into the sea, which represents the nations of the world. I am convinced that the picture here is the same as in Matthew 25:46, which takes place when the kingdom is about to be set up. The wicked will be cast into the furnace of fire and the righteous will remain on the earth for the millennial kingdom.

CONCLUSION

There are several truths we must emphasize as we close this study. (1) This church age is a time of limited success in winning people to Christ, and so we dare not be discouraged when some of the seed does not produce fruit. (2) Since there will be a mixture of good and evil which will continue in the church until God separates the true from the false, we are not to tolerate evil. We are to do everything possible to guard both teaching and life—contend for the faith, but we are not to be contentious—nor dare we usurp the authority of judgment which belongs to God alone.

As we see evil men waxing worse and worse, even in the church, we dare not feel that God's cause is losing ground. We must continue faithfully to attempt to win the lost to Christ, and to bring them into His church under the direction of His Spirit.

9

Matthew 13:53–16:28

━━━━━━━━━━━━━━━━━━━━━━━━━━━━

Training of the Twelve

THE CHAPTER OUTLINED:

INTRODUCTION
THE EXPOSITION
    I. He Faced Unbelief (Matt. 13:53-58)
    II. The Death of John the Baptist (Matt. 14:1-12)
    III. The Feeding of the Five Thousand (Matt. 14:13-21)
    IV. The Walking on the Sea (Matt. 14:22-33)
    V. The Healings in Gennesaret (Matt. 14:34-36)
    VI. Gross Misunderstanding (Matt. 15:1-20)
    VII. Ministry in Tyre and Sidon (Matt. 15:21-31)
VIII. Continuing Healing and Feeding (Matt. 15:29-30)
    IX. The Seekers After a Sign (Matt. 16:1-4)
    X. The Leaven of the Pharisees and Sadducees
       (Matt. 16:5-12)
    XI. The Confession of Peter, the Promise of the Church
       (Matt. 16:13-20)
    XII. The Announcement of His Coming Suffering and Death
       (Matt. 16:21-28)

INTRODUCTION

In many of the Scripture passages which we have studied, we have seen and heard the Lord Jesus as He ministered to the multitudes. This was done largely through His spoken words and through miracles which He performed. Now as the time draws near when He must leave His disciples, He devotes more and more of His time instructing them. They must be prepared for the time when they will carry on His work; hence, we see Him in action as He goes about the business of training the twelve. From these truths, presented so many years ago, there is much for us in our generation, for we, too, must "learn from Him." In this section there are many questions that arise for which we will still search for answers. For example, in the very beginning Jesus makes a simple statement: "A prophet is not without honour, save [except] in his own country, and in his own house" (Matt. 13:57). The question is still with us, "Why?" Or again, "What made Herod think Jesus was John the Baptist risen from the dead?" Then, the Lord gave direction to the disciples concerning the feeding of the 5,000. "Why did He use them in the manner in which He did, particularly when they questioned where He would find food enough to feed such a multitude of people?" "Why did He permit a storm to arise, when He is the master of all creation?" These and many other questions ought to cross our minds as we look at this portion of the Word.

THE EXPOSITION

We have entitled this chapter "Training of the Twelve"; and in reality, after Jesus called them, everything He said and did was part of their training. However now that opposition has definitely come to the surface, we see Him more specifically working with His own apostles. In every circumstance of life, He was carefully showing them (and through them, us), the Heavenly Father, and how as His children we can live in a world of sin, yet live above it.

I. He Faced Unbelief (Matt. 13:53-58)

Jesus went back to His hometown of Nazareth to face those with whom He had grown up. These neighbors and friends had, without a doubt, heard of His miracles and His teaching. Now He returns to share with them directly the same truths—giving them the opportunity to hear and receive His message. He went to the synagogue and began to teach them (v. 54). They immediately sensed something different, authoritative, compared to the teaching of the scribes to which they were accustomed. They could not deny the reports they had heard; hence, they began among themselves to rationalize what He was saying. They questioned (v. 55) concerning His family and their status as a family. It was a carpenter's home, and so had little social standing or even much education. This caused them to ask, "Whence then hath this man all these things?" (v. 56). They had already formed their own conclusions and determined that there was no reason to give special attention to Him. He had been one of them, but had gone far beyond them, hence their jealousy shows through. They were actually offended by Him (v. 57). Notice Jesus in this situation. Without any loss of poise, He answered: "A prophet is not without honour, save in his own country and in his own house" (v. 57). He did not rebel at their unbelief. He simply had given them their opportunity; and when they rejected Him, went His way to other places to continue His teaching and work. There is a great truth in verse 58, that His apostles must also learn; that is, that God does not compel men against their own desire to receive Him or His gracious offer of salvation. We all ought to examine ourselves as to our attitude of rejection. He did not attempt to defend himself, even though He had proved Himself. He simply went on His way. In His parables of the kingdom (Matt. 13), Jesus had indicated that there would be a rejection of His message. This has now begun, and it brings us immediately to this passage where we find Jesus giving a more complete revelation of himself and His work, and predicting His crucifixion and resurrection.

II. The Death of John the Baptist (Matt. 14:1-12)

It will help if we take time to identify Herod the tetrarch, as Herod Antipas, son of Herod the Great. He ruled Galilee and Perea, across the Jordan, throughout the lifetime of Jesus. He is called "king" (14:9), although he did not actually hold that rank. It was the custom of the Romans to refer to their associated rulers in the East as kings, whatever their status. The term "tetrarch" means literally "a fourth ruler." The term was used for one who ruled a part of a total area. At Herod the Great's death his kingdom was divided among three of his sons, and this Herod began his reign about 4 B.C. continuing until A.D. 39. He was the Herod before whom Jesus was later tried.

At this time, Herod spoke to his servants declaring his own belief that Jesus was "John the Baptist; he is risen from the dead." The reasoning back of his conclusion is told in the story in verses 3-12. Sometime prior to this, John the Baptist had dared to tell Herod the truth about his wicked life (v. 4); warning that he should not marry his brother's wife. This bit of advice angered Herod, and had he not feared the popularity of John, would have put him to death immediately. Instead he committed him to jail, and Mark (Mark 6:20) tells us "he [Herod] heard him gladly." However he actually yielded to his own selfish desires, and finally took Herodias as his new wife. This, in spite of the fact he already had a wife. Now, John the Baptist became a threat to both Herodias and Herod. Herodias now was out to "get" John. The occasion of her success was a birthday party Herod gave for himself, to which he invited all of his chief officers and rulers (v. 6). As a feature of the party, Herodias' daughter, Salome, came in to dance for the crowd. It is not difficult to determine the meaning intended by Matthew, for he tells us that "she pleased Herod." Under the influence of the moment, which was a very sensual moment, Herod promised to give Salome whatever she wanted, even to the half of his kingdom (v. 7). The princess (being prompted by her mother) asked for the head of John the Baptist on a platter.

The king was sorry (v. 9), but was caught in his own net. He had John beheaded and delivered to the girl. It must have been quite a moment for her, but only a moment, for she took it to her mother. What an illustration on the part of these three—Herod, Herodias, and Salome—of the perversion of sin and the depravity of man.

The disciples of Jesus came, took up the body, buried it, and went and told Jesus (v. 12). What a word of concern on the part of the disciples, yet, what an illustration—that when sorrow and difficulty come to us, there is One who is always ready to hear and to help—Jesus our Saviour.

III. The Feeding of the Five Thousand (Matt. 14:13-21)

Having learned from the disciples of the death of John the Baptist, Jesus took His disciples and withdrew in a boat to a solitary place (v. 13). He did not panic as men are so apt to do. He did not go out to attempt to do battle with the enemies. He faced the opposition by getting to a quiet place where once again He could share with the Father and receive strength for the future.

But He did not escape the crowds, for they followed Him out of the towns on foot (v. 13). This was the setting for the next great event—the miracle of the feeding of the 5,000. Verse 14 gives us the secret of His life—He saw a great throng of people, and had compassion upon them, and cured their sick. After an all-day ministry, as evening approached, the disciples suggested that He send the people away to buy food for themselves (v. 15).

Here is a lesson for every individual among us—when we get weary and faint, we ought to withdraw and regain strength for ourselves from fellowship with the Father; and then come out again to face the crowds and feed them the spiritual food with which we have been filled. This would once and for all, eliminate the prevalent idea that we cannot do a great job ministering to a multitude. Jesus did, and taught us to do the same. Jesus commanded the disciples to give the crowd something to eat. The disciples knew they did not have sufficient food or money to buy food. They reported only five loaves and two fishes. What limited resources they had—not even enough for the apostles, but they failed to take into account what Jesus could do with limited resources when given to Him. Jesus took the few loaves and two fish, and used them to perform one of the most remarkable miracles of His entire life. He began by commanding the crowd to sit down on the grass, then He gave thanks for the food, broke it, and gave to the disciples to distribute among the multitudes (v. 19).

What an opportunity for application for each of us. Jesus takes what we are and have, when we yield willingly to Him, and then uses us to help meet the needs of the world and to glorify Him. Verse 20 reminds us that there was not only sufficient for the multitude, but after all were filled, there remained twelve baskets full. Those who had distributed to feed the multitudes now gathered up that which was left over, indicating that it is never right to waste the gifts God grants to us. Jesus is teaching and training—and we ought to catch the picture of this miracle which demonstrates for us both Jesus' compassion and His power. They are available to us as we make ourselves available to Him.

IV. The Walking on the Sea (Matt. 14:22-33)

This next section is fascinating in the way Jesus went about to accomplish His Father's will. He sent the disciples across the lake; then He sent the crowd away, in order that He might go up into the mountain to pray (v. 23). It had been a very busy day for the Lord, but here again, He is teaching His disciples—for He went to the mountaintop to pray. There was a crisis just ahead, and He knew the way to gain strength was to wait before the Father in prayer. There is nothing in all the world that can serve as a substitute for the time of prayer. Often the church prayer meeting is called "the hour of power," and it ought to be that. Yet, how few take the opportunity of attending this service of the church. To make it attractive, we have moved to brief moments of prayer, after lots of other things that seem to be more important than the prayer time itself. Jesus surely set a tremendous example, and we shall see it again and again in His life.

The disciples were on their way across the lake, having obeyed the Lord and moved at His command to go on the journey, but a great storm broke upon them (v. 24). Another lesson for them and for us. Storms do break upon all of us, whether we are in the midst of God's will or not. They come upon the unbelievers as well as the believers, but the important thing to see is that they do come to us, even when in the midst of His will. Dr. Ralph Stoll wrote a tremendous tract—*Contrary Winds.* It is an exposition of this passage. In the midst of the storm, "Jesus went unto them, walking on the sea." Matthew announces the hour—it was "in the fourth watch." Dr. Stoll reminds us that Jesus always comes at the right time—"never too early to rob us of the lesson we need, and never too late to bring us deliverance." The hour does not matter to Him, for He knows all about our storms, whether they be in the physical, the mental, the common affairs of life, or the spiritual—and He comes to us. The tragedy is that when He came to the disciples, they did not recognize Him. Often we miss blessings because our eyes are blinded. Then the Lord spoke to them (v. 27): "Be of good cheer; it is I; be not afraid." It would be interesting to trace the idea of "fear not" as a study in God's Book.

At this point, the Apostle Peter gets into the picture by asking for proof that it really was the Lord (v. 28), by bidding Peter to come to Him on the water. The Lord responded very graciously with the invitation "Come." Peter started well (v. 29), but soon got his eyes on the waves and began to sink. At this point, he cried out, "Lord, save me," and Jesus stretched out His hand and lifted Peter up, with a slight rebuke for his little faith. What lessons are here for all of us. There are some who criticize Peter for daring to venture out of the boat, while others look only at the lack of faith and his failure. But to me, it would seem the important lesson in this part of the story is that we can all see much more accomplished for the Lord when we trust Him fully. Remember, this does not imply that we are to be always looking for miracles, for Jesus sent them across the lake in a boat. But when He invited Peter to "Come," it should remind us that His invitation is His promise of power to accomplish. The incident concludes with the disciples filled with awe at Jesus being the Master even of the winds and the waves. They "worshipped him, saying, Of a truth thou art the Son of God."

V. The Healings in Gennesaret (Matt. 14:34-36)

Wherever Jesus went the people flocked to Him to be healed. This is the story of these few verses concerning Gennesaret. Matthew records the fact that they begged Him to let them "only touch the hem of his garment." Then, "as many as touched were made perfectly whole." Does this teach some miraculous power in His clothing? A very clear answer is to be found in Luke 8:46, when in relation to the healing of a woman, Jesus said that when she touched the hem of His garment "virtue" went out of Him. The word used is "dunamis," generally translated "power." This is what healed people.

VI. Gross Misunderstanding (Matt. 15:1-20)

The attitude of the people who lived in Jesus' day can be characterized with one word, *misunderstanding*. We find it emphasized in Matthew 15:10, 16; 16:3, 9, 11-12. We need to remember that the men who became leaders in the conflict were the scribes and Pharisees who were the experts in questions concerning the law. They made a long trip from Jerusalem to ask a very small question about the failure of the disciples of Jesus who transgressed the tradition of the elders, because they did not wash their hands when they ate bread (vv. 1-2). The tradition of the elders concerning the washing of the hands was to avoid ceremonial defilement of the food, and the defiled food would contaminate a man's entire being. In answer, Jesus accused them of voiding God's commandment by their tradition (v. 3). Notice Jesus did not say that tradition in itself was necessarily wrong, but it should not be put on a par with God's Word. Then He gave them a concrete example. A man might have parents dependent on him for financial support. Instead of furnishing them the needed funds, he could declare that the money was devoted to God. According to the tradition of the elders, this man was freed from further responsibility. Though he himself could continue to live on the proceeds of his property, he was by this tradition freed from any obligation to use the dedicated wealth to support his parents. Thus the law had been set aside by tradition. This kind of hypocrisy is not pleasing to God (cf. v. 7). Jesus quoted a passage from Isaiah to seal the meaning of the passage and then urged his hearers to understand what He was saying. He made the application very plain; that when men adopt the doctrines of men, failing to obey God, they worship in vain. Defilement is a moral thing, determined not by what a man eats, nor what he does or fails to do in ceremonial observances, but by those things that come out of his heart (cf. v. 18).

Now the disciples came to Him (v. 12) and reminded Him that the Pharisees were offended at His sayings. These disciples knew something of the power of the Pharisees, and they were fearful of being contrariwise with them. Jesus responded again with composure as He reminded them (vv. 13-14) that there were two kinds of plants in God's garden, and those which the Father had not planted would be uprooted. At this point, Peter asked a question—or asked for an explanation, to which Jesus responded, "Are ye also yet without understanding?" (v. 16). The appeal of the entire section is to a spiritual understanding of the Word of God.

VII. Ministry in Tyre and Sidon (Matt. 15:21-31)

Until this time, Jesus had limited His ministry to Palestine, but now He went to the district of Tyre and Sidon, perhaps into Gentile territory. It would seem evident that He did so for two reasons: (a) To get away from the crowds and particularly the faultfinding Pharisees. (b) He wanted to teach His disciples privately, especially concerning His coming suffering and death. In this new area, a woman approached Him with her problem concerning a daughter possessed of a demon. Her appeal is that of a real concerned parent, for she puts herself in the place of her daughter, and cries, "Have mercy on me." But Jesus remained silent, and in a moment explains His silence to the disciples (v. 24). But before the answer, the disciples came to tell Him that her persistence was annoying to them (v. 23). They did not understand His silence. They perhaps did not recognize that He was testing her faith and adding to her spiritual insight. How often do we fail to understand what seems to be God's failure to answer our prayers in the way that we would like to have them answered? But this woman was an unusual woman. When Jesus paid no attention to her, she did not get angry or leave in disgust. Even when He answered the disciples by reminding them that He was only sent to minister to the house of Israel, she came again and called, "Lord, help me" (vv. 24-25). Then Jesus compared her to a dog, which position she accepted, and said: "Truth, Lord: yet the dogs eat of the crumbs which fall from their master's table." She had met the test, and so Jesus responded, "Great is thy faith: be it unto thee even as thou wilt." And her daughter was healed. The whole incident seems to help in our understanding of the fact that Jesus came to minister to all people; this included the ministry to those who have faith to believe.

VIII. Continuing Healing and Feeding (Matt. 15:29-30)

Jesus now moves into another area near to the sea of Galilee, and into the mountain, where Matthew simply records the healings of many who came to Him—the lame, blind, dumb, maimed, and many others. As a result of the healings, "they glorified the God of Israel." Once again His compassion is mentioned, because they had been with Him for three days without food. Once again the disciples questioned where they would secure food, and once again we see the miracle of Jesus feeding the multitudes. This is a different feeding than the former one, as is attested by the time, place, circumstances, size of the crowd, amounts of food eaten, and of uneaten remains. To attempt to make these two miracles one and the same is to deny the circumstances recorded in the Word. Remember, Jesus was able to do a second miracle— He was not (and is not) limited in the supply of His resources!

IX. The Seekers After a Sign (Matt. 16:1-4)

The Pharisees and the Sadducees were at opposite ends of the pole in what they believed. Now they come together because they have a common cause—their hatred for Jesus. They are opposing Him in His person and work. They are forerunners of present-day enemies of Jesus Christ; those who in many branches of Christendom unite in the doctrine of the Fatherhood of God and the Brotherhood of man. They unite men with differing beliefs, but with one common hatred; namely, the sacrificial death of Christ upon the cross for the sins of mankind. This strange combination of people will be at its height at the coming of Jesus Christ.

These enemies of Jesus came asking for a sign from heaven. He had already done many signs and wonders, and they all knew about these. Think of the present-day opposition and the sudden rise again of occultism; even moving among those who are church members.

Jesus answered the questioners with a sign they all knew about—that of looking into the sky and determining the prevailing weather conditions. Then He reminded them that because they were a "wicked and adulterous generation," they could not understand the signs already given; bringing to their attention the sign of the Prophet Jonah that refers to the death and resurrection of God's Son. Matthew then tells us "he left them, and departed," which are significant words of a significant picture of Jesus removing himself from His critics.

X. The Leaven of the Pharisees and Sadducees (Matt. 16:5-12)

As the disciples were come to the other side, they had forgotten to take bread. Then Jesus warned them of the "leaven of the Pharisees and Sadducees." This caused the disciples to suggest that because they had forgotten to bring bread, He had given the warning. But He quickly corrected their thinking by reminding them of recent miracles of feeding, and then brought their minds from the material to the spiritual. He had to tell them plainly that He was speaking of the leaven which typifies the doctrine of the Pharisees and Sadducees.

XI. The Confession of Peter, the Promise of the Church (Matt. 16:13-20)

We now find Jesus and the disciples in Caesarea Phillipi, where Jesus questions them concerning what men are saying about Him. After the disciples had answered, He asks them the same question ("whom say ye that I am?"), and Simon Peter gives the answer upon which Jesus announces the fact of the future building of His church. Many sermons have been preached on this segment, and most Christians thoroughly understand the importance of the passage. It seems that two things ought to be stressed: (a) That the true church is not built on Peter, but on Jesus Christ Himself. Peter simply made the open announcement that Jesus is "the Christ, the Son of the living God" (v. 16). This was the conviction of the rest of the disciples; however, Peter was the spokesman, just as he was on so many occasions. By designating Jesus as "the Christ," Peter proclaimed that Jesus was the expected Messiah for whom the people were looking. As Jesus accepted the answer, He also announced that "flesh and blood hath not revealed it unto thee, but my Father which is in heaven." The Spirit of God gave Peter the answer, and Jesus pronounced the "blessing." It is the same blessing which Jesus gives to all who believe that He is the Christ, the Son of the living God. (b) The second emphasis of the passage is the promise He made. "I will build my church." This is a new promise, something that He not only will begin, but will continue to do until the church is complete. The church is never named in the Old Testament times, although pictures in type can be found there.

XII. The Announcement of His Coming Suffering and Death (Matt. 16:21-28)

The final verses of this study begin: "From that time forth began Jesus to shew unto his disciples, how that he must go unto Jerusalem, and suffer many things of the elders and chief priests and scribes, and be killed, and be raised again the third day." In this section Jesus makes prediction of His coming suffering, death and resurrection. The nearer we come to the cross, the more deeply we will enter its shadow. He has given Himself now to an increased training of the twelve who will take over at His death.

10

Matthew 17–18

~~~~~~

Signposts on the Road

THE CHAPTER OUTLINED:

INTRODUCTION
THE EXPOSITION
   I. The Transfiguration (Matt. 16:28–17:13)
     a. The Promise (16:28–17:1)
     b. The Occurrence of the Transfiguration (vv. 2-3)
     c. The Conference on the Mount (v. 3)
     d. The Response of the Disciples (vv. 5-6)
     e. The Return to the Valley (vv. 8-9)
  II. The Demon Possessed Boy (Matt. 17:14-21)
 III. A Second Prediction of His Coming Passion (Matt. 17:22-23)
 IV. The Tribute Money (Matt. 17:24-27)
  V. The Greatest in the Kingdom (Matt. 18:1-6)
 VI. Stumbling Blocks in the Way of Children (Matt. 18:6-9)
VII. The Parable of the Lost Sheep (Matt. 18:10-14)
VIII. Treatment of a Brother Who Has Sinned (Matt. 18:15-17)
 IX. Agreement in Prayer (Matt. 18:18-20)
  X. Forgiveness (Matt. 18:21-35)

INTRODUCTION

Near the close of Matthew 16 the Lord Jesus made a significant statement introducing the events that would shortly take place. He frequently had tried to teach His disciples concerning the future, but in 16:21 we read, "From that time forth began Jesus to shew unto his disciples, how he must go unto Jerusalem, and suffer many things of the elders and chief priests and scribes, and be killed, and be raised again the third day."

We begin this section with the study of the Transfiguration. This is followed by another reference to Jesus' death (17:9), and a little later by the second definite prediction of His coming passion (vv. 22-23). Already, those coming epochal events that were to climax His earthly ministry were pointing their shadows across His pathway; hence our subject for the study, "Signposts on the Road."

THE EXPOSITION

The Transfiguration was one of the most climactic moments in Jesus' earthly career. For a relatively short span of time, the three disciples caught a glimpse of the divine glory. As Jesus was in the closest of fellowship with His Father, the eternal glory which is His broke around Him in such a way that the disciples would never forget. The conversation which is recorded for us is very significant. The one thing that concerned Christ and the two heavenly visitors was His coming death at Jerusalem. All the ages had looked forward to the moment of redemption, and all heaven was waiting. Now, it was almost time for it, and there was glory never to be forgotten.

I. The Transfiguration (Matt. 16:28—17:13)

a. The Promise (16:28—17:1). The promise that some of those in Jesus' presence would not die until they saw the kingdom of God at the coming of the Son of Man into His kingdom precedes each account of the Transfiguration. In

Matthew and Luke the chapter division has a way of obscuring the promise from the event, but in Mark they are placed in the same chapter. There have been all kinds of man-made interpretations of this promise. There have been the skeptics, who through it try to prove that Jesus was simply an over-enthusiastic man who believed He would soon establish His kingdom. There have been those who believed that what He really meant was that there were some standing there who would live to see the beginning of His triumph, the establishment of the new kingdom. Some believe that with the founding of the church on the day of Pentecost, Christ actually began to come in His kingdom. However, the fulfillment of the promise is right here in the chapter before us. Peter, one of the three disciples to witness the Transfiguration, wrote concerning it (II Peter 1:16-18).

Within the week after Christ made the promise, Peter, James and John did see the kingdom of God in power, when they beheld the King in His glory, on the mountain. They saw the King in His glory for a brief moment, but we are promised there is coming a day when "every eye shall see him" (Rev. 1:7), and those who are "His" through the redemption which He purchased will be with Him eternally.

The three disciples selected to accompany Jesus on this special occasion were the same as those who were chosen to be with Him at the raising of the daughter of Jairus and in the Garden of Gethsemane. We are not given the reason for this choice; but remember, He is training those who will pick up the work when He leaves the scene of this earth's activities, and each of the three had special tasks to perform. Peter was the leader and spokesman for the group, the preacher on the day of Pentecost, and the writer of two books of the New Testament. James was the first of the apostles to die a martyr's death. John was the one chosen to write five New Testament books, including the Revelation, which tells of Christ in all of His glory. The Transfiguration was but a foretaste.

They were taken "up into an high mountain apart"—by themselves. Many Biblical expositors believe the Transfiguration was at Mount Hermon which rises some 10,000 feet into the air.

b. The Occurrence of the Transfiguration (vv. 2-3). Matthew simply states He "was transfigured before them." The word translated "transfigured" is the same word which is translated "changed" in II Corinthians 3:18. It is the word from which comes our word "metamorphosis." It means a change whereby the form which appears corresponds to the nature within. When Christ was transfigured, the glorious nature within Him which was veiled during His incarnation was allowed to briefly shine through. It was the true nature of Jesus (cf. Rev. 1:13-16), shining through His flesh and His garments, as by a light from within, as the sunlight shining through a stained glass window reveals the true nature of the picture on the wall. This same kind of a transformation is to be the experience of the Christian, according to II Corinthians 3:18. As the believer continually fixes his attention upon Christ as revealed in His Word, he also is changed so that his very outward appearance is made to conform to the new nature within. This is a process for the Christian, to be completed when we see Jesus and become like Him—when we receive our glorified bodies. "And his raiment was white as the light." I am sure that Matthew searched for words to express what really happened, trying to find earthly illustrations that we would understand. It was as though an exceedingly bright light clothed Jesus from head to feet. Alford, the Greek scholar, suggests that "the fashion of his countenance was altered by being lighted with radiance both from without and from within," with a light that never was on land or sea. The glistening of his raiment was "dazzling." The inner light seemed to shine right through his garments. There is only one thing we can conclude; that is, that on this occasion the Lord was covered with that heavenly glory which now clothes Him, and similar to that which will clothe all the saints when our glorified bodies are given to us at the second coming of the Lord.

c. **The Conference on the Mount (v. 3).** This verse tells us that Moses and Elijah came to visit with the Lord and His disciples. It was not a vision, but they were actually present. The disciples not only saw these visitors, but they recognized them in their glorified bodies, perhaps quite like the Lord himself, except nothing is said concerning the radiance. Moses was the representative of the law, which Paul tells us in Galatians was the schoolmaster that leads us to Christ. Elijah was the representative of the prophets who foretold the birth of Christ and prepared the way for His earthly ministry.

These two visitors from heaven talked with Jesus, and the subject of their conversation as reported by Luke (Luke 9:31) was His decease—the word actually is His "exodus," which included His death, resurrection and ascension. These were three of the greatest events in the history of the world, and were the means of the salvation which God has provided for man.

d. **The Response of the Disciples (vv. 5-6).** We do not know how long the heavenly visitors stayed, but when the three disciples saw them departing, Peter spoke out, saying: "Lord, it is good for us to be here." Of course it was wonderful, and it was good for Peter and for us. Peter tells us more about it in his own epistles. We are sure that the experience made the three witnesses better men for the rest of their lives, and the glory which they saw made them realize the value of faithfulness. It increased their faith, and most of all, exalted the Lord Jesus in a manner which they had not seen prior to this time. Immediately, Peter wanted to take action—"if thou wilt"—or are willing, "let us make here three tabernacles" actually "booths" like those used at the Feast of Tabernacles, the great annual Jewish thanksgiving feast. While Peter was speaking, new assurance was given to him, for there came a voice out of the cloud. Peter tells us in his epistle that they definitely heard and understood the voice, and declares that the voice came from the Father. The voice said: "This is my beloved Son," and then added, "hear ye him." There is reassurance in this, yet events that follow show that even after this experience, they did not understand that Jesus must die.

e. The Return to the Valley (vv. 8-9). The two heavenly visitors had gone away, and now the disciples saw Jesus only, and He charged them saying: "Tell the vision to no man, until the Son of man be risen again from the dead." There were perhaps many reasons for this, but since those who had been on the mount with Jesus did not fully understand its meaning, they could not tell it aright. Then if they did not understand, having been with Jesus on the mount, how could others who were not witnesses understand? Furthermore, it would seem to me that the story would make it hard for Jesus to continue His work as teacher and leader, especially if word got around that He was going to die shortly.

There is one very practical application of this final matter of going back into the valley; namely, that those who had been on the mountaintop must again descend into the valley. Christ had given them a commission to carry His message to a needy world. This in reality is a picture of why Jesus came from heaven into the world in the first place—for there was work to be done, and He must come down to earth to do it.

II. The Demon Possessed Boy (Matt. 17:14-21)

What a contrast between these two settings. On the mount we have seen a dazzling display of divine glory, and heard a bit of the conversation with Moses and Elijah. In the valley we look in on a scene of a boy possessed of a demon. His father appeals for help for his son, reminding them that often he falls into the fire and often into the water. The tragedy of the picture is that the disciples had not been able to give him any help. Dr. Gaebelein suggests that this is another passage that has deep spiritual application. The disciples who had been in the valley were a company of believers into whose hands the Lord had put power, and yet they were unable to use that power. Over and over again they attempted to drive out the demons but failure followed them, the crowds jeered them, and the child continued to suffer. It is still true of believers in this dispensation—often we fail because we do not use the power that God has given us. Jesus told the disciples the answer was in their own unbelief, and much of the reason for our failures is our unbelief. Jesus had said that faith could remove mountains, yet we fail so often to exercise faith. He gives the remedy to a lack of faith—"prayer and fasting." Prayer means communion with Christ, and fasting has to do with self-denial. Jesus healed the boy, making him whole, by casting out the demons.

III. A Second Prediction of His Coming Passion (Matt. 17:22-23)

The healing of the demon possessed boy is followed by another announcement of His imminent suffering, death, and resurrection. You will remember that the first prediction followed closely after the announcement of the beginning of the church. This new prediction followed the Transfiguration scene and the tremendous victory over the forces of evil won in the healing of the demoniac boy. It is almost as if Jesus had said that glory can come only through the cross. In His first announcement of His coming suffering, death and resurrection; the chief priests and elders, with the scribes, are mentioned. Here these are not mentioned at all, but He tells His followers that He will be delivered into the hands of men. The disciples again are greatly grieved at His statement; for even yet, they were not understanding what He was saying. Remember He had told those on the mountain with Him, who had seen His glory, to keep silent about it; and so the prediction once again is the cause of great grief. How many in the world today still are in darkness concerning the suffering, death and resurrection of Christ! Do we even understand it after all the years of teaching most of us have received? The story of His suffering ought never to be crossed over lightly in our teaching.

IV. The Tribute Money (Matt. 17:24-27)

The scene of the last six verses of this seventeenth chapter of Matthew shifts once again, and we find it taking place in Capernaum, which actually means "village of comfort." Each year at the end of March every male Jew had to pay a half-shekel (about 35 cents in our money) to the Temple at Jerusalem. The tax collector came to Peter, apparently outside of the house, to inquire about the payment of taxes. Without giving it a second thought, Peter answered yes to the inquiry. Peter then entered into the house, and now the Lord asks a question. He already knew the thought of Peter, because Jesus is none other than the omniscient God, manifest in the flesh. Peter gave Him a correct answer, "Of strangers," to which Jesus replied, "Then are the children free." How could He, the Son of God and the Son of man, pay tribute to the Temple which is already His? But even though He did not really owe any temple tax, He did not insist upon His rights. And, in order that He and the disciples would not be an offence, He gave direction to Peter, the fisherman, to go to the sea and take the first fish that he caught. In its mouth Peter would find a coin which would pay the taxes for them.

A number of things are revealed here, but among the first is the fact that Christ totally identifies himself with His disciples and they with Him. This is His promise to us, that "Lo, I am with you alway." We are partakers of His grace and that includes both His humiliation and His glory. There is another truth which we ought to emulate at all times: He surrendered His personal right for the sake of not giving offence. How often have we said, or at least heard it said: "Well, I have some rights, and I am going to take them regardless of the cost." Even though it may cause some hardship and suffering, as Christians we ought not follow the attitude of the world—demanding our rights.

Then another remarkable thing is to be found in the fact

that the amount was just right for both Jesus and Peter! How many of us spend countless hours of worry about the needs of this life when He has promised to supply all of our needs. How will He do it? I do not know, but our prayer ought to be: "Lord, give me faith sufficient to trust You for the things of this life as well as for the things of eternity." We trust Him for eternal life, but we worry for ourselves concerning the present life. How foolish!

V. The Greatest in the Kingdom (Matt. 18:1-6)

There is no break in the continuity of thought between this chapter and the events of the last one. They ought not to be divided even by a chapter heading, for it is a continuation of thought. "At the same time," the disciples came to Jesus with their question: "Who is the greatest in the kingdom of heaven?" After a tremendous lesson on making no offence, they were thinking only of themselves! Once again, Jesus very patiently uses a visual aid to give them a clear answer. The disciples were questioning concerning the kingdom as they understood it; that kingdom which was and still is to be established on the earth, and they wanted their own rights in that kingdom. The Lord took a little child as an example for His teaching. The kingdom must be entered by way of a new birth, and that means a complete turning around from the way the natural man is going. A new life must be given and must be entered by a spiritual birth just as a child comes into the world by a natural birth. He did not say that Christians ought to be "childish," but rather childlike. There is a vast difference. Childishness says—I want to be first, I always want my own way; but a childlike characteristic is shown in a life where there is growth and development. It is a life of utter dependence and self-forgetfulness. Jesus is saying to His disciples that we need to lose unfounded confidence and pride. Remember the Heavenly Father must occasionally take His children to the woodshed; even as He admonishes earthly fathers to do with their children. Jesus said that the way of true greatness is to become as a little child.

VI. Stumbling Blocks in the Way of Children (Matt. 18:6-9)

This may be interpreted as referring to young believers; the young and inexperienced in the Christian life. "Offend" simply means "cause to stumble into sin, to hinder in their Christian lives." To get the full impact of our Lord's words here, we must keep them in context. Jesus is impressing upon us the fact that to keep a child from coming to Christ, or from growing in Christ is to offend Christ himself. To hinder or harm a child spiritually, Jesus says, is such a terrible thing that it would be better to die even a violent death than to be guilty of this sin. God is declaring the importance of the spiritual life as compared to the physical. We are very careful in our society to see that children are protected in the physical realm, but too little thought is given to the emphasis upon the spiritual. As a matter of fact, the Lord suggests that it would be far more beneficial to an individual to perform physical surgery upon various parts of the body than to allow those parts to offend.

VII. The Parable of the Lost Sheep (Matt. 18:10-14)

The continuity of the chapter continues as Jesus proceeds with His definite training of those who would pick up His work. He defined His major objective among men; namely, "the Son of man is come to save that which was lost," and illustrated it with the parable of the lost sheep. Since this is covered more fully in another Gospel, we only place it before you to be sure to include the importance of reaching the lost.

VIII. Treatment of a Brother Who Has Sinned (Matt. 18:15-17)

How many problems would be solved in the church if the instructions given here were carried out by all of its members. These are very plain directions on the "How To," in dealing with a brother who has wronged us. Do we "tell him his fault between thee and him alone"? (v. 15). Or do we tell everybody else? The wisdom of taking along a witness for the second interview, if the first fails, has often been demonstrated. For your own sake and the sake of the church, you may need an additional voice of testimony to your own as to what was or was not said. Frequently, the individual who will not listen to reason when you approach him is liable to be a troublemaker at every instance—hence the protection is suggested. It all falls into proper sequence in this chapter. If a brother sins, we should approach him as though he were a little child, remembering that we too were in sin, and Jesus Christ forgave us and brought us into the family of God.

IX. Agreement in Prayer (Matt. 18:18-20)

Knowing the difficulty of this kind of action concerning a brother, the Lord moves to give instruction on a pattern of prayer. He sets before the assembly of believers both the privilege and responsibility of prayer. Whatever the thought is of binding or loosing men's souls by our failures is indeed a solemnizing thought.

X. Forgiveness (Matt. 18:21-35)

The remaining verses of our study comprise another answer of the Lord—this time in regards to the subject of forgiveness. In the previous portion of the discourse, Jesus had referred to offenses which led others to sin, and had been teaching the disciples what to do when others trespassed against them. This responsibility seemed to bother Peter, and the answer seemed difficult for him to perform, particularly since it was so contrary to the thinking of the day. Thus we see Peter asking the question: "How oft shall my brother sin against me, and I forgive him?" He intimates by the question that his brother is expected to sin again. Is seven times of forgiveness enough? But Jesus responded, "Until seventy times seven." The answer is not a mathematical formula, but rather a principle for continuing forgiveness.

In the story which follows, Jesus told of a man who had been forgiven a tremendous debt of ten thousand talents—

estimated to be somewhere between ten and twenty million dollars in our money. An amount which he could never possibly have paid. Yet this same man—a servant—refused to forgive a fellow servant a small obligation of perhaps twenty dollars. Dr. R. W. Dale, a writer of a former generation, once said: "Many Christian men have given a new turn to this text. In their own private interpretation of the New Testament, they have rewritten it to read: 'whosoever speaketh a word or committeth a wrong against God, it shall be forgiven him; but whosoever speaketh a word or committeth a wrong against me, it shall not be forgiven him.'"

Jesus taught us to pray: "Forgive us our debts, as we forgive our debtors." Fortunately for most of us, He is a far better forgiver than are we. We ought to learn from God's forgiveness of our sins, how we also should forgive.

From this study on signposts along the way, let us learn that in an era of unforgiving spirits, God still forgives and forgets and would teach us to do the same.

11

Matthew 19—21:11

━━━━━━━━━━━━━━━━━━━━━━━━━━━━━

Jesus' Last Journey to Jerusalem

THE CHAPTER OUTLINED:

INTRODUCTION
THE EXPOSITION
   I. The Question of Divorce (Matt. 19:3-12)
      1. Jesus' teaching on marriage (vv. 3-6)
      2. Jesus' teaching about divorce (vv. 7-8)
      3. Divorce and remarriage
  II. The Blessing of the Children (Matt. 19:13-15)
 III. The Rich Young Ruler (Matt. 19:16-22)
 IV. The Danger of Riches (Matt. 19:23-26)
  V. The Rewards for Consecration (Matt. 19:27-30)
 VI. The Parable of the Laborers in Vineyard (Matt. 20:1-16)
VII. The Third Prediction of His Coming Suffering (Matt. 20:17-19)
VIII. The Ambition of James and John (Matt. 20:20-23)
 IX. The Triumphal Entry (Matt. 21:1-11)
      a. The Preparation for the Entry
      b. The Procession

INTRODUCTION

As the title of this chapter indicates, we now give ourselves to the study of Jesus' last journey to Jerusalem. Ahead lay the cross and the empty tomb. Jesus began His ministry in Judea, but the greater part of it was spent in Galilee. There He taught in the synagogues, on the seashore, and on the hillsides roundabout. Great crowds followed Him wherever He went. He made a number of trips to Jerusalem for the various festivals of the people which were held in the city. Now He is going on a journey that will bring death to Him, and through the gate of death, resurrection, and finally the ascension to His Father and home. Some very important issues are dealt with as He continues to teach His disciples in preparation for the work they will soon be called upon to carry on.

THE EXPOSITION

After Jesus left Galilee, on His way to Jerusalem, multitudes flocked to hear Him. As was His custom, He stopped to teach them the will of God. Soon the Pharisees were there to continue their testing of Him.

I. The Question of Divorce (Matt. 19:3-12)

Although Jesus has spoken on this subject, there are still many who are seeking to find a way around what He said. Notice, this is exactly what the Pharisees were doing as we begin this nineteenth chapter. The record says they were "tempting him," which means they did not come to learn the truth, but to find a way around that truth, and if possible to get Him into trouble. His answer gives us some of the most wonderful revelation concerning marriage and divorce found in all the world. It would be far easier to neglect this portion since we are dealing with the trip to Jerusalem, but He gives us the information on marriage and divorce while He is on the way to His death; hence, we do not disregard it.

1. Jesus' teaching on marriage (vv. 3-6). There is much said in the Bible concerning the matter of marriage, and here in response to the question of the Pharisees, Jesus took time to set the record straight. Marriage is a very serious business, and Jesus actually used the union of man and woman in marriage as a glorious picture of His own union with the church (cf. the Book of I Corinthians). They questioned Jesus about the matter of divorce, but He responded by talking first about marriage. Marriage is the oldest institution known to man. Jesus said: "Have ye not read, that he which made them at the *beginning* made them male and female." Marriage was founded in the Garden of Eden, and the first wedding was performed by God when He gave Adam a helpmate in the person of Eve. Marriage is older than the church, the state, or the school. The purpose of the union of man and woman in marriage is for the formation of the home which is the foundation of all human society. Marriage is of God and is designed for the happiness of man and woman. God regards the marriage vow as a sacred covenant, made before Him, and a contract for a holy partnership. It is not just a civil ceremony to be entered into as a legal contract, but rather, a gracious provision of God. When this union is performed, then the wife must come first with the man. She must come before parents, friends or business. The same applies to the wife, for the husband must have first place in all relationships.

2. **Jesus' teaching about divorce (vv. 7-8).** After this discourse on marriage the Pharisees were not satisfied, so they came back with the question: "Why did Moses then command to give a writing of divorcement, and to put her away?" Without doubt, they referred back to Deuteronomy 24:1-2. When the Pharisees claimed that Moses "suffered" them a bill of divorcement, Jesus answered that Moses did indeed permit divorce. But He immediately emphasized the fact that this was a concession because of the unwillingness of the people to live by God's declared will. In Moses' day, the people had just come out of sinful Egypt where all manner of gross sin was a way of life. The Israelites got involved in this same way of life and were living in unfaithfulness and adultery; so Moses

provided for legal divorce, in order to control an evil practice which already existed. Moses allowed divorce because of the hardness of the hearts of men.

So, too, divorce today is only a refusal on the part of mankind to abide by the rules and standards which God has revealed. Moses permitted it, but from the beginning it was not so. God has not changed His rules, and divorce is not according to God's will. If the hearts of men of Moses' day had been tender and full of love, there would have been no desire for divorce. In the final analysis, all sin is a rebellion against God and a lack of love for Him and our fellow men.

3. Divorce and remarriage. In the same story as told in Mark's Gospel, the disciples were still not satisfied completely, and when they came into the house, they asked Him to spend a little more time discussing with them the problems involved. Now (v. 9 ff), there is added the matter of remarriage. It begins with a definite statement by Jesus: "I say unto you, Whosoever shall put away his wife, except it be for fornication." This last clause has been the subject of debate for many years; and I am sure we will not settle it, with a few words here, to the satisfaction of all who study this portion of Scripture. The best way to settle the argument is to accept what it says—and abide by it. Actually, the real controversy is not over divorce at the moment, but rather over the possibility of the so-called innocent party remarrying. To the best of my knowledge, there is no other passage in the Bible that gives the right to remarry, except where there is the death of one partner; and then, of course, the contract is concluded and the party who remains is free to marry. The question of this section of study is not concerning salvation—but rather of a human relationship, the highest relationship of mankind—that of marriage and its sacredness. The church surely is duty bound to teach its people concerning this even though it may not be easily accepted. I am sure that God in His infinite wisdom and grace can forgive the sin of disobedience in this area of life, as much as in any other area; but those involved must surrender their lives to Christ, and subject their wills to Him in every decision that is made.

II. The Blessing of the Children (Matt. 19:13-15)

Notice at this point the reaction caused by the bringing of little children to Jesus. The command given to Adam and Eve in the garden was to "replenish the earth," and of course that replenishment meant children. What a tragic note is upon us at every turn in the road as we see children that are being deprived of their rightful kind of environment in which to be reared. They should have the privilege of a happy homelife, which is the result of a happy union of father and mother.

In these verses we find that parents brought their children to Jesus so He might place His hand of blessing upon them and pray for them. Jesus rebuked His disciples for their apparent lack of concern for children. Actually, not to care for children is a bad commentary on the character of an individual. Jesus certainly put His approval on the bringing of children to Him by concerned parents. It is an attitude that ought to be promoted.

III. The Rich Young Ruler (Matt. 19:16-22)

The next few verses tell us of an interview between Christ and a young man who was certainly a good man by the moral and social standards of the world. However, he needed salvation, which indicates that regardless of our position in life, or our wealth, the most important matter is that of salvation. Two other gospel writers (Mark and Luke) tell of this interview and give us the same essential story, each adding additional details.

We know from the story that this young man believed the Scriptures, for he knew that he had *need* of eternal life. He was a good moral man, and as Jesus questioned him, he replied that he had kept the commandments. Without doubt he had his faults, and these were well known to Christ; however, looking at it from a man's viewpoint his moral conduct was satisfactory. He was a ruler in Israel; probably ruling in things of religious life rather than political. But there was something missing in his life, and he knew it as he came running to Jesus and knelt before Him. He immediately inquired what he must do to inherit eternal life. He wanted to be saved, but he eventually turned away.

Where did he fail? He came to Jesus, and addressed Him as "Good Master," because he believed Him to be a religious teacher; but he did not accept Him as his Lord and Saviour. He knew that in spite of his religious exercises, and his keeping of the commandments, he did not have eternal life. He was dissatisfied, and he longed for satisfaction. Jesus responded with a question: "Why callest thou me good? there is none good but one, that is, God." He said in essence—either I am not good, or I am God. Once again, He was adding evidence of His equality with the Father, so that the disciples could have additional basis for their own faith. The young ruler did not fully understand the law, or he would never have said, "All these things have I kept from my youth"—for notice that he selected to name those commandments which most moral men keep. He failed to mention his keeping of the law which had to do with God. Then he asked, "what lack I yet?"

Many individuals today still believe that the way to eternal life is by what they do, when in reality, Jesus has done it all. Jesus put His finger on the real problem by suggesting that the young ruler forsake his earthly riches and surrender his life to Christ. The young ruler did not receive Christ, but turned away from the Saviour and continued to follow his idol—the riches of this life.

IV. The Danger of Riches (Matt. 19:23-26)

This action opened the door for Jesus to further teach concerning the danger of riches. His statement must have come like a bombshell to the disciples, for it was commonly held that wealth was a sign of God's distinct favor. Let us not misunderstand the problem. The disciples did, and it caused Jesus to quickly explain that He meant that the difficulty was not the riches, but that people often "trust in riches" (v. 24). This is why riches become such a handicap to salvation. It is not that wealth is wrong, unless it is gained in wrong methods, but it is so easy to put trust in wealth and what wealth can do for us. When Jesus used the "eye of the needle" as an illustration, He was talking about a human impossibility. To enter the kingdom of God in any way other than through Christ is an impossibility, but God in His gracious provision has made it possible. Man cannot save himself, and a rich man is less inclined to seek favor from God, for often he feels self-sufficient. Can a rich man then be saved? Of course, in exactly the same manner as a poor man.

V. The Rewards for Consecration (Matt. 19:27-30)

This entire conversation led naturally to the next incident in which Peter asked—in that they had left all—what would they get? Does Peter sound a bit mercenary? Are we ever guilty of the same kind of approach? The Lord Jesus very gently overlooked the self-centeredness of Peter and assured him of abundant reward. A hundredfold and eternal life also. The eternal life is God's gift, and the hundredfold is the reward. Really wonderful dividends for whatever Peter invested. Read the promises that the Lord has made to all those who serve Him. The books of the New Testament are full of these promises.

VI. The Parable of the Laborers in Vineyard (Matt. 20:1-16)

Although this is not included in the portion of the thirteenth chapter of Matthew concerning the parables, it fits in the account as a parable on the same subject that Peter had just asked about—"What do I get out of all my hard labor?" The great truth of this story ought to serve as a warning to all of us, not to be too greedy about material things—money and the like. Which comes first—service or its pay? It also teaches that length of service is not the answer to the amount of the reward. I wonder what would happen in the world today if the kind of pay were meted out to workers as in this story. Jesus laid a real principle down when He reminded those who complained, that it really was His prerogative to give to those who labored in any way according to His own desires, as long as He paid that which He had bargained to pay to those who worked throughout the day.

VII. The Third Prediction of His Coming Suffering (Matt. 20:17-29)

In the midst of all of this, the Lord took His disciples aside and again made the prediction of His suffering and death. There is a new element added now; namely, that He would be betrayed to the chief priests and scribes, and that they would condemn Him to death and deliver Him to the Gentiles to mock, to scourge, and to crucify. Then on the third day He would rise again. Note how carefully the Lord had prepared the disciples prior to this time, and now He adds the full prediction—even as to method. None of this was new to Jesus, but the disciples were amazed and fearful as they followed Jesus to Jerusalem.

VIII. The Ambition of James and John (Matt. 20:20-23)

The procession is halted momentarily with a request coming from the lips of the mother of James and John. Once again, it is self-seeking ambition that comes to the forefront. Jesus had once spoken of the fact that those who followed Him would occupy 12 thrones and judge the 12 tribes of Israel. Perhaps this word impressed itself upon this mother and upon the 2 sons, James and John. For a mother to desire a place of honor for her sons seems to be such a natural thing, and the sons knew enough about the entire matter to be ambitious, also. This request, coming on the very threshold of the parable Jesus had just spoken concerning the workmen in the vineyard, makes it that much more difficult to understand the disciples.

Jesus replied by reminding them that they would have to drink of the cup which He would shortly drink, but to give these places was not His to give, but rather belonged to the Father. What a kind answer, even though they did not understand what He had meant concerning the cup that He would soon drink. They answered in the affirmative without knowing the depths of His sorrow and suffering, but they would soon know.

Here is one question that might be raised—Is the Son not equal with the Father? He had claimed this on numerous occasions, but now He says He does not have the authority to give honored positions to anyone—that is the Father's privilege. The answer is again to be found in the fact that when Jesus came to the earth, He laid aside some things, one of which was this authority to give. We ought not to see in this answer any hint of inferiority of Jesus to the Father.

The healing of the blind men is the closing scene of the chapter, and it takes place as Jesus and the disciples are departing from Jericho, followed by a great multitude. This healing is one of the last miracles of healing recorded by Matthew. These two men cried unto Jesus, addressing Him as "Lord, thou son of David." The multitude rebuked them for calling on Him, and many believe their rebuke came because of identification of Jesus as "son of David." However, He "had compassion on them" and healed them. Dr. Gaebelein again reminds us that there is dispensational truth to be gleaned here, for the two blind men sitting by the wayside groping the darkness become types of the remnant of Israel in the end of the age. That remnant will cry to Jesus as Son of David and call upon Him for deliverance. The two blind men were healed, and they followed Him. Their eyes were suddenly opened, even as the eyes of Israel will be opened to sing praises to the Lord.

IX. The Triumphal Entry (Matt. 21:1-11)

The Triumphal Entry into Jerusalem is celebrated by Christians on Palm Sunday. However, there is strong evidence that this short trip from Bethany to Jerusalem occurred on Saturday. For those who would remind us that this would mean the breaking of the law of the Sabbath, let us remember that the Scripture itself tells us that the distance from Bethany to Jerusalem was a Sabbath day's journey (Read Luke 24:50 and Acts 1:12).

a. **The Preparation for the Entry.** Although it is often suggested that the Triumphal Entry was a sudden response of people to Jesus, and that they were totally unprepared for it all, let us be reminded that all of it was the result of definite planning by the Lord. He knew exactly what He wanted to do, and He followed the procedure to the very end. In verses 2 and 3, Jesus sent 2 of His disciples into the village where "ye shall find an ass tied, and a colt with her: loose them, and bring them unto me." The two of them being tied together would help the disciples know they had the right animals. Both were to be brought. The directions were very explicit and showed His omniscient and regal character by His foreknowledge of these details and the authority of His command. "The Lord hath need of them" is very significant. At no other time in all of His ministry do we read of Jesus riding from place to place. The inference was that He usually walked, often with great crowds following. Now He sends for an ass and the foal of an ass to ride the short distance from the Mount of Olives to Jerusalem. This was more than a physical need, as Matthew explains in the next verses (4-5), "that it might be fulfilled which was spoken by the prophet." Zechariah 9:9 gives us the promise that the King would come "having salvation; lowly, and riding upon an ass, and upon a colt the foal of an ass." The ass did not particularly represent, as so often suggested, "lowliness," but rather royalty. It was the custom for kings to ride on asses when they came on missions of peacefulness. If on horseback, it indicated war. Jesus was coming into Jerusalem on the beast of royalty, and yet He was lowly in His very manner of appearance. He wore no regal robes and was accompanied by no members of the royal court. He came now to make a public claim of messiahship, using the symbolic sign predicted by Zechariah 9:9, which Israel well knew. The disciples who were sent, did exactly as they were commanded; and when they had found the ass, and the foal, they put their clothes upon them, and sat Jesus upon them (cf. vv. 7-8).

b. The Procession. "A very great multitude spread their garments in the way; others cut down branches from the trees and strawed them in the way" (vv. 8-9). Some of the disciples had already thrown their garments over the back of the animals, now others spread theirs on the ground making a pathway for Christ and those who followed. This act indicated humility and allegiance to the One they were honoring. The very tense of the verb indicates repeated action, which suggests as the animals passed over the garments, those in the rear of the procession picked them up and put them down again ahead of the procession. They also cut branches from the trees and spread them along the way.

The crowd cried, saying: "Hosanna to the son of David: Blessed is he that cometh in the name of the Lord; Hosanna in the highest" (v. 9). Each of the writers of the story record some of the proclamations made on the journey. "Hosanna" means "save now," and was perhaps drawn from some of the phrases of Psalm 118:25-26, which was one of the Psalms recited by the people at some of the great feasts of Jerusalem. As you watch the actions now, and those that transpired in a short while, you cannot help but wonder how much of the Psalm, or anything else, these who followed really understood.

The willingness of the owner of the animals to give them to the Lord when the disciples said: "The Lord hath need of them," ought to be an example to all of us. We ought to ask ourselves—Is our property at Christ's disposal if He has need of it? This would include our homes, our automobiles, our money, as well as our time and energy to get the Gospel out.

We celebrate the day of the entrance of Christ into Jerusalem as the Triumphal Entry, but that is somewhat misleading. Jesus did ride in triumph toward Jerusalem, and in the final analysis it was a step toward His final triumph which is yet to come. For that moment at least, it might better have been called the "DAY OF REJECTION," for it was a day given to the Jews to receive Jesus as the Messiah. But Israel rejected Him. There was but one alternative—the crucifixion. It might well be called the day of "LOST OPPORTUNITY."

12

Matthew 21:12–25:46

━━━━━━━━━━━━━━━━━━━━━━━━━

Passion Week Activities

THE CHAPTER OUTLINED:

INTRODUCTION
THE EXPOSITION
  I.   The Cleansing of the Temple (Matt. 21:12-17)
  II. The Withered Fig Tree (Matt. 21:18-22)
  III. Teaching Again in the Temple (Matt. 21:23–23:39)
       a. "By what authority doest thou these things? and who gave thee this authority?" (21:23)
       b. The question of paying taxes (22:15-22)
       c. The question of marriage and the resurrection (22:23-33)
       d. The question of the Pharisees (22:34–23:13)
  IV. Teaching on the Mount of Olives (Matt. 24–25:46)
       a. General picture of the age while the kingdom is in mystery (24:1-8)
       b. The Great Tribulation (24:15-28)
       c. The coming of the Son of Man (24:29-31)
       d. Practical principles in parables (24:32-51)
       e. The ten virgins (25:1-13)
       f. The parable of the talents (25:14-30)

INTRODUCTION

If you knew that you had approximately one week of life ahead, and then life on this earth would come to a conclusion—how would you spend that week? Rather a foolish question; for no one knows whether he has a week, a day, or a minute. But Jesus knew the end from the beginning, and He knew that He was now moving very swiftly to that moment when He would commit His spirit back to the Father.

THE EXPOSITION

Where would you expect Jesus to go as He came to the city of Jerusalem?

I. The Cleansing of the Temple (Matt. 21:12-17)

Perhaps a better title for this section would be "Activities in the Temple," although we generally put the emphasis upon the cleansing of the Temple. Matthew adds several other items which we look at briefly. "He went into the temple" (v. 12). Mark indicates that on the first day of entry into the city, Jesus went to the Temple and looked around without a word. On the next day He returned and performed the act of cleansing it of its moral and spiritual evils. At the end of His ministry, He did that which He had done at the beginning (John 2:13-17).

The court of the Gentiles was the Temple market where animals, oil, wine, and other items essential for sacrifices and Temple worship were sold for the convenience of pilgrims who came from all parts of the world to offer sacrifices, especially at the Passover season. The priests made gain out of the traffic and there was opportunity for extortion. You can almost imagine the noise, confusion, wrangling, bitter words, dishonest practices that filled the court where those who came should have been taught God's law and way. "Tables of the moneychangers"—these were necessary because the pilgrims came from all over the civilized world. However, because of their evil practices of extortion and robbery, Jesus cast them out and reminded them of the Old Testament prophecy: "My house shall be called the house of prayer; but ye have made it a den of thieves." Once again, He exerted His kingly power by destroying the works of the great enemy, Satan. There seems to be a very practical application that needs to be made; namely, Jesus would have us stay about the main business for which He gave His life, the ministry of salvation for the lost.

Likewise, "the blind and the lame came to him in the temple; and he healed them." Often we slip over this phrase, but it is a part of the total picture of His ministry. To talk about casting out those who made merchandise in the Temple is not sufficient. We must likewise share the ministry of doing good. Mercy upon the helpless is just as much a part of His ministry as stern justice which He has just performed.

Then another group is introduced into the record, "the chief priests and scribes" saw and heard the things which He had done, and they heard the children who were still crying in the Temple, "Hosanna to the son of David." The children had been on the march with Him, and they had not changed their opinions of the Saviour as rapidly as did the elders of the crowd. They are still singing praises unto the Messiah. This angered the chief priest and the scribes ("they were sore displeased"—v. 15). They asked Jesus to put a stop to the loud praises. His reply was (v. 16): "Have ye never read, Out of the mouth of babes and sucklings thou has perfected praise?" (cf. Ps. 8:2). With this statement, Jesus now left and went out of the city to Bethany, to lodge there (v. 17).

II. The Withered Fig Tree (Matt. 21:18-22)

Early in the morning, as He was on His way back to the city, "he hungered." So often, there is so much in so few words. He was the King of kings, but now He hungers. By the side of the road He saw a fig tree; but when He came to it, He found it bearing nothing but leaves—no fruit. His declaration was: "Let no fruit grow on thee henceforward for ever." This caused the disciples to marvel and ask questions. Once again Jesus calls attention to the importance of their faith, so great power is available that even the mountain itself can be cast into the sea (cf. vv. 20-21). In the Word of God, the fig tree is well known as a type of Israel, and the cursing of this tree is the illustration of the national rejection of the people of Israel. They had yielded no fruit, therefore the barren tree was cut off while the roots remain. There is, of course, the other truth which ought to be stressed. The mountain to which Jesus referred is a picture of a great obstacle which Jesus reminds us can be removed by faith and prayer. Notice the word "limited" in Psalm 78—"and [they] limited the Holy One." Illustrations are plentiful concerning how Israel limited God, and it is also true of us in our generation—we limit the Almighty.

III. Teaching Again in the Temple (Matt. 21:23—23:39)

Once again Jesus has gone into the Temple. He is teaching the people, and without doubt a great multitude has gathered. Of course the enemies came also to oppose Him. These enemies are now making ready for the final confrontation, and they ask a series of questions:

a. "By what authority doest thou these things? and who gave thee this authority?" (21:23). On their last confrontation "they were sore displeased," and that displeasure does not heal easily. Now they are back at it again, only in a bit different fashion. Now they are questioning His authority. He answered their question by asking one of His own about John's baptism (vv. 24-25). They were in a dilemma, for John had been the one to announce Jesus as the Son of God, the One who had come to be the Saviour of men. If they admitted that John's baptism was from God, then why hadn't they received Him about whom John had preached? If they would have denied this baptism as being from heaven—and said from men—the multitude would have turned their backs upon them. They discussed it among themselves and finally answered, "We cannot tell." They knew, but they lied! Then Jesus answered and said, "Neither tell I you by what authority I do these things." They knew that He had claimed to be the Son of God, and that He had cleansed the Temple in the name of His Father.

Then He gave them a parable in the story of a man who had two sons, and he gave command to the first son to work in the vineyard, and the son refused; but later changed his mind and went. The second son said: "I go, sir: and went not." Then a very searching question as to which of the two sons did the will of his father? They knew, and now answered correctly. Jesus made the application, verses 28-32. The King had acted as a judge in the case, and by their own statements pronounced them guilty. The truth that ought to be sounded here is that mental assent, even verbal willingness is not sufficient. The action of obeying the Father's command is more important than the word of mouth.

Then comes a second story in which Jesus reviews the history of their nation, and predicts the coming calamity (vv. 33-40). When Jesus talked of the vineyard, they must have known that He was referring to Israel. The story is founded upon Isaiah 5:1-7, and other Old Testament passages which speak of the same thing. The vineyard has provided no fruit. The servants who came to the vineyard are the prophets whom God sent, and they were mistreated and rejected. Finally the Son came, and now He is standing in their midst. What will they do with Him? Will they yield to His authority and receive Him? No, He replied, they will cast Him out of the vineyard and kill Him. They responded that the King will destroy those wicked men and give His vineyard over to other husbandmen. The Lord again had won the battle. They had spoken their own condemnation, and so the Lord quoted from the twenty-second verse of Psalm 118. Then the Lord spoke the words of doom for Israel in verses 43-44. They need no exposition, only belief that He will do what He has promised to do. They would like to have finished the job right then and taken Him, but "they feared the multitude because they took him for a prophet" (vv. 45-46).

Immediately, He gives them another parable (22:1-14), often called the "parable of the Wedding Guest." Once again the words so familiar in the thirteenth chapter begin this parable, "The kingdom of heaven is like unto"—which identifies the subject matter immediately. The wedding feast is for the Son, and in His honor. The invitation was sent out to the special guests, that is, to Israel. The servants sent out were to tell those invited "that all things are ready." But they would not come. Then other servants were sent out to repeat the invitation (vv. 4-5). Even though these who were bidden had brought Him to the cross, another opportunity was given; but they made light of it, going about their regular tasks as if nothing had happened. Then the King sent forth His armies, destroyed the city and the murderers. This was the end of God's dealing with Israel for the moment—that is, for the present age. However, this does not mean that the individual Jew is rejected. He can still hear and accept the Gospel of Christ and be saved. Now more servants are sent out with invitations; however, there was one requirement, they must have on the wedding garments. The Lord Jesus himself has provided the robe—a robe of righteousness, not of our own, but which He himself has provided. Without it, men will be cast into outer darkness, even as the one who had come to the feast without the garment.

b. The question of paying taxes (22:15-22). The Pharisees now call for help from the Herodians (v. 16), and they came with a question concerning paying taxes—tribute to Caesar. Jesus asked them a question concerning the tribute money and gave a great principle of life: "Render therefore unto Caesar the things which are Caesar's; and unto God the things that are God's." What an answer—and they left and went their way.

c. The question of marriage and the resurrection (22:23-33). The Sadducees did not believe in a resurrection; hence,

138 □ **Studies in Matthew**

they came to attempt to catch Him in their trap. Quickly He saw through their scheme and gave them a statement signifying that Abraham and Isaac and Jacob were not dead, but alive, and that God is the God of the living. The multitude heard and were astonished.

d. The question of the Pharisees (22:34—23:13). Their question concerned the law and which was the greatest commandment. He responded that the first commandment was to "love the Lord thy God with all thy heart, and with all thy soul, and with all thy mind [understanding]. . . . And the second like unto it, Thou shalt love thy neighbour as thyself." This baffled the questioners, and well it might, for God was the giver of the Law in the first place. Then the Lord had a question of His own for the Pharisees, "What think ye of Christ?" This was a question they could not—or would not—answer.

The chapter closes with Jesus pointing out the hypocrisy of the Pharisees and pronouncing a series of woes and judgment upon them.

IV. Teaching on the Mount of Olives (Matt. 24—25:46)

The next teaching recorded for us is often called the "Olivet Discourse" because it was given on the Mount of Olives. It is the only discourse found in all three Synoptic Gospels, and is the second longest discourse revealed to us from the lips of Jesus. As Jesus and His disciples left the Temple area where He had been teaching and climbed the rise of the Mount of Olives, the disciples talked of the splendor of the Temple. A beautiful sight to behold as it is described. The buildings themselves decorated with costly articles donated by the people. The disciples were proud of this Temple and told Jesus about it. He answered by saying that those stones which seemed so secure would be cast down and not one left standing upon another. This brought from the disciples a series of questions: "When shall these things be? and what shall be the sign of thy coming, and of the end of the world [age]?"

a. General picture of the age while the kingdom is in mystery (24:1-8). Jesus did not answer directly as to the time for the end of the age, nor when these things would occur; but He did at this point describe the characteristics of the age and warn His followers to watchfulness. Jesus took time to give this instruction concerning events preceding the end of this age.

1. "Many shall come in my name, saying I am Christ" (v. 5). Let us remember that the first seal of Revelation 6 produced the rider on a white horse, a picture of the Antichrist. In Matthew 24:5, the first item mentioned is the coming of many who will claim to be Christ, of whom the final one will be the Antichrist.

2. "Wars and rumors of wars" (v. 6). The second seal of Revelation tells of warfare by the rider on the red horse. This verse tells of wars and rumors of wars.

3. Famines are the next in the list of Matthew's account (24:7), and the third seal of Revelation to be opened pictures a black horse and the rider with a pair of balances.

4. Great natural catastrophes, such as pestilences and earthquakes that will occur, follow the famine. The fourth seal brings death over the fourth part of the earth.

5. The fifth seal tells of the martyrs slain during this period, and Jesus told the disciples that "then shall they deliver you up to be afflicted and shall kill you" (v. 9).

This section in Revelation deals with the period after the church has been raptured, and the seventieth week of Daniel has begun. It seems reasonable therefore to see this section of Matthew as referring to the same timetable. Often these things are preached as signs of the times in the present hour, and the application of such, I believe, does not do harm to the Scriptures. But we have not seen anything yet, nor will the believer see these things in fulfillment, for they come after the rapture. The disciples had some light on these predictions for many of the writers of Old Testament prophetic truths had said similar things, and the disciples were already acquainted with these prophecies. These prophetic truths will be fulfilled before the coming of the King and the establishment of His kingdom.

The section concludes with two verses that have often been taken out of context and misapplied in various ways. "But he that shall endure unto the end, the same shall be saved" (v. 13), has often been used in reference to the task of the Christian who must persevere to the end, in order to receive salvation. However, we know that salvation is "by grace . . . through faith," and that faith is in Jesus Christ the Saviour. The statement of Jesus must be kept in the context which has just preceded it. Verses 10-12 tell us of that awful day of suffering for the Jews when they shall betray one another and shall hate one another. A day when false prophets will arise and deceive many, and others will grow cold in their perseverance. But to those who endure, there will be salvation.

Verse 14 does not teach, as so many have interpreted it, that the world must be evangelized before Christ can return. The verse does not refer to the gospel of grace, but rather to the gospel of the kingdom, which is the announcement of the coming of the kingdom which will occur at the return of Christ. This message will be carried to all nations by the sealed remnant of Israel (cf. Rev. 7).

b. The Great Tribulation (24:15-28). Verse 15 definitely fixes the time that the following things will happen, "the abomination of desolation, spoken of by Daniel the prophet." The prediction is found in Daniel 9:27 in the prophecy of the seventy weeks. The abomination is said to occur at the middle of the seventieth week and has reference to the worship of the Jews. During the first part of this week, the Antichrist will be in league with the Jews; but now at the middle of the week, he breaks covenant with them, and brings all manner of heartache and sorrow to them. Revelation 13 describes these events. You may want to refer to this chapter, although there is so much right here to consider. An important matter to keep in mind is found in verse 21, "great tribulation, such as was not since the beginning of the world to this time." The most horrible picture we can draw will be nothing compared to the reality predicted by the Lord.

c. The coming of the Son of Man (24:29-31). The return of Christ with His saints will come at the end of the tribulation and will usher in the kingdom age; and during this period, all the promises of God to Israel will be fulfilled. At the beginning of these days, Israel will have some sort of a sign that Jesus is the Messiah, and Zechariah aptly described it thus: ". . . and they shall look upon me whom they have pierced, and they shall mourn for him as one mourneth for his only son . . ." (Zech 12:10).

d. Practical principles in parables (24:32-51). The parable of the fig tree is simply that fruit and leaves are here together. As soon as the branch becomes tender the fruit is found. It is a rapid development. So with Israel as they are given the blessing; new life, fruit and glory will be quickly realized in those end days. For further light on this, read Dr. A. C. Gaebelein *Gospel of Matthew.*

There is a problem with the use of the phrase: "This generation shall not pass, till all these things be fulfilled" (v. 34). It is very evident that not all of these things were fulfilled during the lifetime of the disciples. Some events await the Great Tribulation and the coming again of Christ, this time in all of His glory. The word translated "generation" may, and we believe does in this case, refer to a race, or family. Hence, the meaning is simply that the Jewish race will continue to exist until the end of the age. God is not finished with them in His program, and even the persecution of the tribulation will not bring an end of this people. Then Jesus speaks a very strong word concerning His Word, and the fact of the passing away of heaven and earth—but not His Word. He will make good on all of the promises recorded in both the Old and New Testaments.

There is, however, not to be an actual release of the timing. Verse 36 reminds us that even though the disciples wanted to know the exact time of these events, only the Father knew. Jesus had laid this knowledge aside with His glory while He sojourned upon the earth. In continuing His description of His coming in glory, we must continue to interpret in light of these things "after the tribulation," with an exhortation to "watch."

There is one other error that is put aside in this section—the interpretation of verses 40-42. Often it is interpreted that one is taken to heaven while the one left had missed the rapture. Not so, for this is at the time of His coming in power and glory—and immediately before it—the one taken from the field, and the one from the mill are not pictures of the church at the time of the rapture, but of some being snatched away to judgment, and others being left to enjoy the blessing.

e. The ten virgins (24:1-13). There are two interpretations of this parable either of which can claim the names of very godly men for their particular interpretation. The first is the group that believes this has reference to the church. The virgins are said to represent the professing members of the church who are awaiting the return of the bridegroom. The oil is the picture of the Holy Spirit who indwells all true believers, but is not possessed by the professing Christians. When the cry is given at midnight for the virgins to go out to meet the bridegroom, only those who have the oil can attend the marriage.

The second interpretation applies this parable to the Jewish remnant just as the content of the previous chapter. The wise virgins are those Jews who have genuinely prepared for Christ's coming by responding to the Gospel during the tribulation. The foolish virgins are the Jews who only profess to believe during that period. When Christ returns to the earth with His Bride, the Church, only the genuine believing remnant will be permitted to meet Him and enter into the wedding feast and the kingdom. I believe the context demands this second interpretation. The first stage of the marriage of Christ and the Church, His Bride, came following the rapture of the Church into heaven. Heaven is His and our home during the period of the tribulation. When He comes back to the earth with His saints after the tribulation, He is bringing His Bride with Him to His home and to the final celebration of the wedding feast (v. 10).

There are many ways in which the ten virgins are alike, or at least similar. They were all virgins; they all went forth, which means they had the same religious profession. They all had lamps, indicating some enlightenment. There was a real difference, however: one group had a form of godliness, but without Christ; they had knowledge without obedience; they had a religious experience without justification. They all slumbered and slept, the difference being one group had oil, that is, the Holy Spirit indwelling them—the other did not.

Regardless of your interpretation, there are several practical applications:

1. We should always look for the coming of the Lord.

2. We should always be ready.

3. We should never omit the doctrine of the second coming of Christ in our thinking, teaching or preaching.

There is a word that tells it all: WATCH.

f. The parable of the talents (25:14-30). The emphasis of this entire parable is on the principle of rewards. Let us all be reminded that works never bring salvation, but they do prove whether or not the faith is saving faith.

g. The judgment of the nations (25:31-46). This closing portion of Jesus' teaching has to do with judgment—not of individuals, but of the nations. Actually, the word here translated "nations" is translated 64 times "nations," and 93 times "Gentiles." Judgment is on the basis of their treatment of the Jews.

Christ is concluding His training of the twelve. There is yet much to be done, and we see it in the next chapter.

13

Matthew 26–28

The Suffering, Death and Resurrection of Jesus

THE CHAPTER OUTLINED:

INTRODUCTION
THE EXPOSITION
   I. The Conspiracy Against Jesus (Matt. 26:1-5, 14-16)
  II. Christ in the Upper Room (Matt. 26:17-35)
     a. The Preparation for the Meal (vv. 17-19)
     b. The Gathering at the Table (vv. 20-26)
     c. The Institution of the Bread and the Cup (vv. 26-30)
     d. "When they had sung an hymn, they went out . . ." (v. 30)
     e. The Prediction of Peter's Denial (vv. 31-35)
  III. Christ in the Garden (Matt. 26:36-46)
  IV. The Betrayal and Arrest in the Garden (Matt. 26:47-56)
   V. The Jewish Trial (Matt. 26:57-68)
  VI. The Denials by Peter (Matt. 26:69-75)
 VII. The Roman Trial (Matt. 27:1-26)
VIII. The Crucifixion (Matt. 27:27-50)
  IX. The Resurrection of the King (Matt. 28:1-10)

INTRODUCTION

We have come in our study to the very heart of the Gospel. Now we see Jesus, the sinless Son of God, who became a man for our sakes, dying as the sacrifice for our sins and rising again as the final proof of His Lordship. This study of the Book of Matthew is the record of Jesus' life beginning in Bethlehem with the incarnation. He was taken for a brief time to Egypt to escape the decree of Herod and then brought back to live in Nazareth. From there we followed Him to the Jordan for His baptism and into the wilderness of Judaea for His temptation. Then He returned to Galilee for the greater portion of His public ministry. We followed with Him across the Lake of Galilee where He performed a number of miracles; including feeding of the multitudes and the healing of many people. He then traveled to Caesarea Philippi and to Tyre and Sidon. From there we came with Him on His last journey to Jerusalem where we discover the major part of our present study. Until now, we have watched Him through a little more than 33 years of life. The largest part of our Scripture passage covers approximately 24 hours—one long day in His life and that of His disciples. Then of course, most of the twenty-eighth chapter of Matthew refers exclusively to the day of the Resurrection.

THE EXPOSITION

I. The Conspiracy Against Jesus (Matt. 26:1-5, 14-16)

The paragraph begins with a meeting of Jesus and His disciples in which He gave some thought to preparation for the Passover, and with it a very important announcement concerning His betrayal (v. 1). The important message at this point for us is that He was not caught unaware of the plot that was organized against Him.

In another place (v. 3) there was a group meeting, including "the chief priests, and the scribes, and elders of the people." These people met with the high priest, Caiaphas, and consulted together how they might take Jesus by subtility and kill Him. They, of course, faced a problem, for it was near the feast day, and they knew they dared not do it on the feast day for fear there would be an uproar of the people. Their plot as to how it might be done was given a boost when (v. 14ff) Judas Iscariot came into the meeting asking them to pay a price to him, that he might betray Jesus. The price offered was 30 pieces of silver; and the scheme was in operation.

Meantime, back in Bethany with Jesus and the disciples, a woman came with a gift of precious ointment contained in an alabaster box. She poured the ointment on the head of Jesus, and His disciples became indignant, suggesting that this was terrible waste when it might have been sold and proceeds given to the poor. In John 12 we have the woman identified as Mary, the sister of Martha. There are many lessons to be learned from the story of the anointing among which are (a) this most costly gift represented the best she had, and she saved none for herself; (b) the odor of the ointment filled the house, and so the acts of devotion which we bring to the Lord will continue to bring blessing to those with whom we share. (c) The greatest lesson is, without doubt, the heart occupation of Mary with her Lord. She was not much interested in what was going on around her, nor even in the criticism of those who brought it upon her. The Lord was the object of her faith and her devotion. When the church gets this much involved in showing their love to the Lord, the mouths of the critics will soon be stopped.

Who did the complaining? The Gospel of John intimates that Judas Iscariot was the leader of the criticism and quickly influenced some of the others. But Jesus answered those who criticized with words of appreciation for Mary's service. He suggested that her act would be remembered; and surely, the very words of this part of the chapter are still being remembered by us today.

II. Christ in the Upper Room (Matt. 26:17-35)

Many people mistakenly refer to the scene of this paragraph as the last Passover of which Jesus partook. It is more correctly called the "Last Supper," and John clearly suggests this in John 13:1, "Now before the feast of the passover." Later that evening when Judas left after receiving the sop, verse 29 suggests because Judas had the bag, "that Jesus had said unto him, Buy those things that we have need of against the feast." The Passover feast was still future at the time of the trials which occurred early the next morning. The actual crucifixion took place on a preparation day, and this preparation was for the Passover (cf. John 19:31).

a. **The Preparation for the Meal (vv. 17-19).** The day before the feast required a great deal of preparation. Every Jewish family diligently searched through the house in order to remove every bit of leaven that could be found. The leaven was burned and the unleavened cakes were prepared for the feast. Remembering that the Jewish day began at six o'clock in the evening, this event took place on Tuesday evening. The details of the preparation made ahead of time indicate that although Jesus knew He would not eat of the Passover, He gave the disciples command to make the preparations without revealing the time of His death, a fact which He did not desire to disclose at the moment.

b. **The Gathering at the Table (vv. 20-26).** At the eventime He sat down with the twelve (v. 20). Remember, the Passover was to be eaten with shoes on, and standing in commemoration of the original Passover (cf. Exod. 12:11, 25). Matthew very clearly tells us that "he sat down with the twelve," therefore, this could not have been the Passover. While they were eating the meal, Jesus said, "one of you shall betray me" (v. 21). The Lord knew who the betrayer would be. Earlier in His ministry He had shown that He knew the true character of Judas (cf. John 6:71). Judas had already been with the chief priests and scribes, and the bargaining had been completed. Now Judas was awaiting the opportunity to make the final arrangements to bring it to a conclusion. Of course this very open statement on the part of Jesus brought surprise to the apostles, and every one of them began to say unto Him, "Lord, is it I?" (v. 22). Jesus answered, "He that dippeth his hand with me in the dish, the same shall betray me" (v. 23). This bit of food offered to Judas was, in essence, a final loving gesture by the Lord to Judas, the betrayer, and it pointed out his identity. With it the Lord gave a further word, "woe unto that man by whom the Son of man is betrayed" (v. 24). This, in spite of the fact that the death of Christ had been predicted in the Old Testament, and even the matter of betrayal by an associate had been pictured in Psalm 41:9.

Judas was not under compulsion to betray Jesus, nor is he released from the awful sin which he committed. The sin itself is foreseen in the Word of God, but responsibility for sin is the result of his deliberate choice. Judas now responds by saying, "Master, is it I?" He knew that he had already bargained to betray the Lord, but perhaps to cover up his sin, and to remove any thought on the part of the disciples that he would be guilty of the sin, he asks the question. Sin adds to itself in an attempt to cover up sin.

c. The Institution of the Bread and the Cup (vv. 26-30). John 13:30 tells us that he (referring to Judas) "having received the sop went immediately out: and it was night." We now have the record of the institution of the "Eucharist," which comes from the Greek word *eucharisteo,* and is the word for "give thanks," and the word "Eucharist" is often applied to the symbols of the bread and the cup. The impact of the entire eucharist is that these elements were given as symbols to portray the basic truths of our redemption, and they serve as constant reminders of these truths. The bread as a symbol of His broken body, and the wine, referred to as "the cup," the symbol of His shed blood. Both Luke and Paul give us the fact that Jesus instituted this rite as a *reminder* that the Lord desires to be remembered for His sacrificial death on the cross.

d. "When they had sung an hymn, they went out . . ." (v. 30). This of course does not give the complete record of all that transpired in the upper room that night, but it is that part which Matthew describes for us. The singing of a hymn, without doubt, would have been one of the Psalms with which they were all familiar, and it brought to a conclusion the fellowship of that hour in an upper room.

e. The prediction of Peter's Denial (vv. 31-35). Matthew does not reveal to us where they were nor how quickly after the singing of the hymn before Jesus picked up the conversation, but He did pick it up. This time it was the prediction of the scattering of the apostles, of Peter's denial, and of Jesus' own resurrection and that He would go before them into Galilee. Peter quickly responded in his own self-confidence and his own strength: "Though all men shall be offended because of thee, yet will I never be offended" (v. 33). This should be a warning to everyone of us, never to boast in ourselves, but always to be dependent upon the Lord and to move in His strength. Peter said it a second time, after Jesus had definitely told him of the denial—this time even adding to the first statement: "Though I should die with thee, yet will I not deny thee." But do not be too harsh on Peter—for Matthew tells us, "Likewise also said all the disciples." How easy it is to take a stand for the Lord in the midst of others who take the same stand, but when the enemy moves in, how often it becomes an easy gesture to move with the crowd so we can save our own popularity, or even our own physical well-being. The movement of the rest of the apostles seems to me to be another illustration of the influence leadership has even through the very words which we speak, and a challenge to be careful of every spoken word. In the next few circumstances we will watch carefully to discover how well they kept their pledge to Jesus.

III. Christ in the Garden (Matt. 26:36-46)

From the upper room, they moved directly to "a place called Gethsemane" (v. 36). The Lord, with perfect calmness, chose a place that was well known to the disciples, including Judas. He was actually making himself available at this moment to those who would bring Him to trial and death. Once again, He took three of the apostles with Him into the garden a bit farther than the others. Why He took this action is not revealed to us anywhere in the Word, but we have seen these three together with Him on other occasions (at the raising of Jairus, and on the Mount of the Transfiguration). It is my personal conviction that they were to have special work to do in their later ministries, and now He is but preparing them for this work. To the eight, He had said: "Sit ye here, while I go and pray yonder." To the three, He said: "My soul is exceeding sorrowful, even unto death: tarry ye here, and watch with me." The full meaning of "watch with me" is "stay awake and watch," a command that might be given to those who would stand guard over the camp when the enemy is close at hand.

"He went a little farther, and fell on his face, and prayed, saying . . . if it be possible, let this cup pass from me . . . " (v. 39). There have been many suggestions as to just what He was saying at this moment in His life. Some have suggested that He was shrinking from the awful physical suffering and death which He knew were just ahead, but we must remember that He knew the only way of salvation was through this suffering and death; hence, He would not now deviate from His purpose. Some others have suggested that Satan was trying desperately to keep Jesus from the cross, and would now try to kill Him in the garden, thus avoiding the cross. But Christ knew that He would not die until His hour had come, and then His death would be voluntary. Therefore Satan could not kill Him in the garden, so this interpretation is not the answer.

Dr. Merrill Unger has given a clear statement that I believe is the interpretation of the passage. He says:

This [the cup] involved no fear of death, but the contact of His sinless soul with the sin of the whole world as its vicarious Bearer and Expiator through the death on the cross (Isa. 53:10; II Cor. 5:21). This was the cup He prayed might pass from Him, but only in the Father's will. His was an infinite anguish, as His infinitely holy soul faced the ordeal of "being made sin" and knowing the prospect of the hiding of the Father's face.

How wonderful to know that the request in the garden was closed by a voluntary subordination of the Son's will to that of the Father. If there was no other way for Him to be the sin-bearer than to experience the forsaking by God for a time, He was willing to do so for us. He came out of the inner garden and saw the three asleep. Note that Jesus directed the conversation towards Peter: "What, could ye not watch with me one hour?" You promised that you would stay by, even though all others would flee. Then He added a second word of direction to the three: "Watch and pray, that ye enter not into temptation: the spirit is willing, but the flesh is weak." The prayer was the same as before, then He returned back to them, and again, found them asleep—"for their eyes were heavy." He did not awaken them but went away again and prayed the third time, using the same words. He returned and said to them: "Sleep on now, and take your rest." Sleeping apostles in an important hour like this! We might be guilty of saying—How thoughtless and careless can they be? But are we guilty of the same—sleeping through great blessings and opportunities that are at our finger tips? The hour had come, and now Jesus said: "Rise, let us be going: behold, he is at hand that doth betray me."

IV. The Betrayal and Arrest in the Garden (Matt. 26:47-56)

Judas, one of the twelve, came, and with him a great multitude (cf. v. 47). The traitor must have gone directly from the upper room to bring back with him a group of people including priests, temple officers, and a multitude of the curious who came along to see what was going on. One has suggested that the reason for the multitude was that perhaps the Jewish authorities arranged a large group in order to make it appear that Jesus was really stirring up a rebellion, and therefore was a very dangerous person. Judas gave the prearranged sign, saying: "Whomsoever I shall kiss, that same is he; hold him fast." Judas approached Jesus and kissed Him. He spoke likewise and said, "Hail Rabbi," at which point Jesus identified himself by saying, "Friend, wherefore art thou come? Then came they, and laid hands on Jesus and took him." Jesus did not resist; He was the master of the situation. One of the disciples (identified by John as Peter) impulsively started swinging with a sword. This act identifies Peter as being a very courageous man, attacking to attempt to protect the Lord. He succeeded in severing a servant's right ear. Luke reminds us that Jesus healed the man, and incidentally, this is the last miracle recorded where Jesus is said to have healed a man (see the account in the twenty-second chapter of Luke). Jesus commanded Peter to put away his weapon, and then reminded them that if He should call upon legions of angels they would protect Him; but the Scriptures could not then be fulfilled. Then a very tragic note which tells us simply that now, "all the disciples forsook him and fled" (v. 56). This was the fulfillment of the prophecy of the Lord that they would forsake Him.

V. The Jewish Trial (Matt. 26:57-68)

Apparently Christ had been taken first to Annas following His arrest (cf. John 18:12-13). This was not an official trial hence the Synoptic Gospels do not record it. Caiaphas was the son-in-law of Annas and was high priest because of Roman influence. These two were associated together in the traffic among the Temple merchants. They are said to have held a monopoly for the selling of animals of sacrifice at the Temple, and thus were involved in political corruption. They "sought false witness against Jesus, to put him to death" (v. 59). Even here, the false witnesses could not agree in their charges, which should have been sufficient to throw the case out of "court" and release the prisoner. The fact that the trial was occurring in the nighttime was a violation of their own law; but they finally apparently found at least two would agree, and so they accused Him of blasphemy (v. 61). In all of the accusation, Jesus had remained silent.

The high priest asked the question recorded here (v. 63), in order to get something tangible which they might use to condemn Jesus. Now He would either have to deny the claims of His ministry, or else would admit that which would seal His doom before that court. Jesus responded, "Thou hast said," which was an affirmative admission of His deity. He also added that there was coming a time when the whole scene would be reversed. Then He would not be the accused, He would be the judge on the throne; and the Jews who knew of Daniel's prophecy knew that of which He was speaking. This angered them beyond words, and the high priest "rent his clothes, saying, He hath spoken blasphemy" (v. 65), and the crowd "spit in his face, and buffeted him" (v. 67). This simply means that the first to bring physical violence upon Jesus were members of the Sanhedrin. To vindicate themselves of their violence, they called upon Him to prophesy unto them, naming the one that had smote Him (cf. v. 68).

VI. The Denials by Peter (Matt. 26:69-75)

These verses record the fulfillment of the prediction of Jesus concerning Peter who was so boastful just a few hours prior to this time. The last record was that they all had forsaken Him and panicked when He was arrested. Peter had attempted to protect with his sword, but the Lord had given command to put up his sword, which he did. Then he ran, and so did all the others. But he comes back into the picture now, and at verse 69 we discover him sitting in the palace court where he could watch what was going on. When questioned, he said he didn't know what they were talking about (v. 70). Then Peter attempted to leave and had gone out into the porch, and another maid questioned him upon which he made his second denial and accompanied it with an oath. A little while later, others came to him with accusations (v. 73) of being one of Jesus' followers, and Peter made his third denial of being a part of the followers, "began to curse and to swear, saying, I know not the man." The first denial led to the second, and the second to the third; each time it became a bit easier, and this time he cursed and swore. Then the prophecy was fulfilled, because "immediately the cock crew" (v. 74). Peter remembered—and repented. Luke tells us that at that moment, Jesus turned and looked at Peter. How important to know that Jesus is still watching us, and a look into His Word will reveal our sin. As the Christian repents of his sin, he is promised cleansing.

VII. The Roman Trial (Matt. 27:1-26)

It is the morning hour, and those who had determined to put Him to death were following what they purposed (vv. 1-2). They bound Him and led Him away to the Roman governor, Pontius Pilate.

At this moment, Judas sees that they are going beyond what he thought they would do, and he is regretful for his part in the act. The word translated "repented himself" is not the same word generally used for repentance, but is a word that means "regretful." He brought back the "blood money," tried to give it back to the chief priests, and really threw it down at their feet with the confession that he had sinned. The chief priests took the money and bought a burial ground which is called "the field of blood." Judas left— and committed suicide. It is a picture of the terrible remorse of a lost man! He knew there was ahead of him the eternal punishment which Jesus had talked about so often.

Now Pilate questioned Jesus (vv. 11-14). "Art thou the King of the Jews?" And Jesus simply responded, "Thou sayest." Then the chief priests and elders began again their accusation, and He never answered them. This caused the governor to marvel and to wonder how he could get out of all of this. Then there came the way of escape—verse 15 tells us there was a custom that the governor release a prisoner of the people's choice. He named one that might become involved, "Barabbas." He gave them their choice—Jesus or Barabbas!

VIII. The Crucifixion (Matt. 27:27-50)

Volumes have been written on the crucifixion. Sermons by the multitude have been preached and lessons taught. Let us carefully reread the words from the Bible, allowing the Holy Spirit to speak to our hearts as we remember that He was drinking the cup—suffering the wrath of God for the sin of the world as He took our place on the cross for our sin. Who crucified Christ? The answer is found in John 10:18— "no man taketh it from me, but I lay it down of myself."

Accompanying the death of Christ there were many disturbances which Matthew records, including (a) darkness (v. 45); (b) veil of the Temple rent (v. 51); (c) and an earthquake which rent the rocks and opened graves (vv. 51-52).

IX. The Resurrection of the King (Matt. 28:1-10)

The Sabbath ended at six o'clock Saturday evening—He had been in the tomb three days and three nights and just before daybreak on Sunday, the first Easter, Jesus came out of the tomb. Verses 2-4 tell of the stone which had sealed the tomb and which is now rolled away. We read of the testimony of the angel (vv. 5-7), and the meeting of Jesus with the women (vv. 8-11). We also read the record of the unbelief and opposition that were still prevalent (vv. 12-15). But the entire story of His earthly life is not ended. He arose, and is victorious over sin, death, and the grave.

He remained on the earth—coming and going to meet with the disciples; and finally in the last few verses of this great book, He gives to the disciples and to us, the great commission and the promise to be with them and us until the end of the age. We are assured of this, because all power is given unto Him, both in heaven and in earth.

Can we conclude in any greater manner than to say: "Hallelujah—What a Saviour!"

In 1958 Congress passed the Food Additive Amendment, including the Delaney Clause, which clearly states that additives should be banned if they induce cancer in laboratory animals. Unfortunately, however, the amendment does not apply to additives that were in use before it was passed, so, since nitrite and nitrate had already been in use for a long time, they were automatically included on the list of chemicals "Generally Recognized as Safe." To complicate matters further, nitrite in meat is regulated by the USDA, while nitrite in fish is under the jurisdiction of the FDA. And these agencies generally leave it to industry—the profit-maker—to determine whether or not an additive is safe. The final irony in this long list of governmental errors is that the FDA depends heavily, for "independent" research and advice, on the food committees of the National Academy of Sciences, which Daniel Zwerdling claims are "like a Who's Who of the food and chemical industry" (Verrett and Carper 34).

Nevertheless, as they have come under fire in recent years on the subject of nitrite and nitrate, the FDA and the USDA have found it necessary to give reasons for their continued sanction of these chemicals. First, they find fault with the experiments done to date. According to the USDA, for example,

> The Department was aware that under certain conditions, nitrites do interact with secondary amines to form nitrosamines and that some nitrosamines are carcinogenic. However, knowledge in this area was limited and analytical methods available to study the possibility of nitrosamine formation in meat food products containing the permissible amount of sodium nitrate lacked the necessary accuracy and reliability to give conclusive results (Verrett and Carper 152).

Despite the Delaney Clause, moreover, the FDA points out, "Man is the most important experimental animal and nitrites have not been linked to cancer in all the years that man has been eating the chemical" (qtd. in Wellford 179). This is an almost foolproof argument, since cancer usually shows up only after its inception, and it is extremely difficult to trace it to any source. And certainly it is unlikely that any sizable group will offer to serve as guinea pigs for nitrite experiments. In evaluating this argument, it is significant that humans are generally more susceptible to chemical damage than animals—ten times more so than rats, for example (Verrett and Carper 59). Following through on its own logic, however, since nitrite has indeed been proven to cause cancer in dogs, the FDA has dutifully and responsibly banned its use in dog food.

The industry's second argument is that nitrite prevents botulism. However, the USDA regulations approve the use of nitrite and nitrate only as color fixers. If they are being used as preservatives, this is a new use and comes squarely under the auspices of the Delaney Clause, which would have them banned outright because they cause cancer in animals.

The last argument is that small enough doses of carcinogens are not dangerous. Dr. Leo Friedman, director of the FDA's Division of Toxicology, puts it this way:

> . . . There is always a threshold level below which the substance does not exert any physiologically significant effect. . . . The design of a safety evaluation study is to determine a level at which there is no demonstrable effect. This level, when divided by a suitable safety factor, is then considered to be a safe level, in that there is a practical

certainty that no harm will result from the use of the sub-

stance at that level.   (Qtd. in Wellford 180)

The medical community does not agree. The Surgeon General's committee

stated in 1970, "The principle of a zero tolerance for carcinogenic ex-

posures should be retained in all areas of legislation presently covered

by it and should be extended to cover other exposures as well" (Wellford

181). Hughes Ryser stated in the New England Journal of Medicine:

". . . weak carcinogenic exposures have irreversible and additive ef-

fects and cannot be dismissed lightly as standing 'below a threshold of

action.'" He also commented that, until the carcinogens are removed

from the environment, "efforts must continue to educate populations and

government about their presence" (qtd. in Wellford 181). Even with

this, the FDA Commissioner, Charles Edwards, strenuously disagrees: "We

can't deluge the public with scare items based on our suspicions. . . .

The pendulum swings too far in most cases, and consumers tend to boycott

a product . . . even though we might feel that continued use within cer-

tain limits is entirely justified" (qtd. in Wellford 18).

     Something has gone wrong. The issue is one of what we eat. It

makes no sense at all to eat a substance until it is proven to be poi-

son. Even a starving man is reluctant to eat mushrooms unless he knows

what he's doing. Nitrite is banned altogether in Norway, and forbidden

in fish in Canada. European allowances are generally lower than

ours, and even the Germans make their "wursts" without nitrite.

     One is forced to a radical conclusion. The American government is,

in this instance, clearly serving the interests of the industry rather

than the people. The fact is that the food industry is willing to spend

millions every year to make sure the regulatory agencies act in ways

that please them. Each time an additive is banned, the food industry

finds itself in the spotlight. It feels an implicit threat to all its other additives, and ultimately to the immense profits Daniel Zwerdling

describes:

> This marvelous chemical additive technology has earned $500
> million a year for the drug companies . . . and it has given
> the food manufacturers enormous control over the mass market.
> Additives like preservatives enable food that might normally
> spoil in a few days or a week to endure unchanged for weeks,
> months, or even years. A few central manufacturers can satu-
> rate supermarket shelves across the country with their prod-
> ucts because there's no chance the food will spoil. Companies
> can buy raw ingredients when they're cheap, produce and stock-
> pile vast quantities of the processed result, then withhold
> the products from the market for months, hoping to manipulate
> prices upward and make a windfall. (22)

Under pressure from the food industry, and probably influenced as

well by a sincere, if hazy, patriotic optimism, the FDA issued a fact

sheet in May 1967, stating unequivocally that our soil is not being poi-

soned by fertilizers, that pesticide residues are entirely safe, that

our soil is the "envy of every nation," and that food processing is a

"modern marvel because the natural value of the food is not lost in the

process." It concludes, "Today's scientific knowledge, working through

good laws to protect consumers, assures the safety and wholesomeness of

every component of our food supply." The FDA's continuing support for

nitrite allowances, despite increasing evidence that nitrite is lethal,

indicates that the FDA has not removed its rose-colored glasses.

A recent extended discussion, The Health Effects of Nitrate, Ni-

trite and N-Nitroso Compounds, issued in 1981 under the auspices of the

National Academy of Sciences, offers no new information but by saying

that nitrites in cured meats may be no more harmful than those in vegetables, baked goods, and cereals, it seems to suggest that cured meats may be less dangerous than has been thought. Still, as Marian Burros pointed out in the New York Times, many specialists feel that The Health Effects offers no new evidence. And in fact, an even more recent study by a committee organized by the National Academy of Science strongly implies (Assembly 12) that the government should develop a safe alternate to nitrites.

Until the FDA and other regulatory agencies begin to see clearly, then, the American consumer has little choice other than to give up eating the nitrited cured meats and smoked fish on the market today. If we do so, we will be following the practice of Dr. William Lijinsky, a biologist who has studied the problem for fifteen years. "I don't touch any of that stuff when I know nitrite has been added" (qtd. in Sheraton 18).

Modern Language Form

Works Cited

Assembly of Life Science. <u>Alternatives to the Current Use of Nitrite in</u>

    <u>Food</u>. Washington: National Academy Press, 1982.

Hunter, Beatrice Trum. <u>Fact/Book on Food Additives and Your Health</u>.

    New Canaan, Conn.: Keats, 1972.

Jacobson, Michael F. <u>Eater's Digest</u>. Washington: Center for Science in

    the Public Interest, 1982.

Robbins, William. <u>The American Food Scandal</u>. New York: Morrow, 1974.

Sheraton, Mimi. "Take Away the Preservatives, and How Do Meats Taste?"

    <u>New York Times</u>, 13 June 1985, p. 26.

Verrett, Jacqueline, and Jean Carper. <u>Eating May Be Hazardous to Your</u>

    <u>Health</u>. New York: Simon and Schuster, 1974.

Wellford, Harrison. <u>Sowing the Wind</u>. New York: Bantam, 1973.

Zwerdling, Daniel. "Death for Dinner." <u>The New York Review</u>, 21, No. 1

    (21 Feb. 1974), 22-24.

    ————. "Food Pollution." <u>Ramparts</u>, 9, No. 11 (June 1971), 31-37,

    53-54.

SYMBOLS COMMONLY USED
IN MARKING PAPERS

All instructors have their own techniques for annotating essays, but many instructors make substantial use of the following symbols.

ab   faulty or undesirable abbreviation (see page 704)

agr   faulty agreement between subject and verb (page 480) or between pronoun and antecedent (page 479)

apos   apostrophe (pages 702–03)

awk (k)   awkward

cap   use a capital letter (pages 699–700)

cf   comma fault (pages 682–84)

choppy   too many short sentences—subordinate (pages 492–95)

cl   cliché (pages 464–65)

coh   paragraph lacks coherence (pages 94–97); sentence lacks coherence (pages 472–82)

cs   comma splice (pages 682–84)

dev   paragraph poorly developed (pages 82–88)

dm   dangling modifier (pages 476–77)

emph   emphasis obscured (pages 490–501)

good   a good point; or, well expressed

frag   fragmentary sentence (pages 497–98, 680–82)

id   unidiomatic expression (page 718)

ital   underline to indicate italics (page 698)

k (awk)   awkward

Lewis Thomas, "On Natural Death" ___ ___ ___
Henry David Thoreau, "The Battle of the Ants" ___ ___ ___
Lester C. Thurow, "Why Women Are Paid Less
    Than Men" ___ ___ ___
E. B. White, "The Door" ___ ___ ___

7. Do you think the professor should continue to assign this book next

    year? _____

    Did you tell her or him? _____

8. What would you have us change next time? _____

    _____

    _____

9. May we quote you in our promotion efforts for this book?

    _____Yes _____No

_____

Date   Signature

_____

Mailing address

3. Were the exercises useful? _____

4. Did you like the examples? _____

5. Please give us your reactions to the following readings:

	Keep	Drop	Didn't read
Martin Luther King, Jr., "Nonviolent Resistance"	___	___	___
Bruce Catton, "Grant and Lee: A Study in Contrasts"	___	___	___
E. B. White, "Education"	___	___	___
Margaret Mead and Rhoda Metraux, "On Friendship"	___	___	___
Jonathan Miller, "The Body in Question"	___	___	___
Anonymous, "Eclipse"	___	___	___
Sylvia Plath, "The Journals of Sylvia Plath"	___	___	___

6. Please give us your reactions to the additional readings in Part Four

	Keep	Drop	Didn't read
Russell Baker, "The Flag"	___	___	___
James Baldwin, "Stranger in the Village"	___	___	___
Robert Benchley, "How to Get Things Done"	___	___	___
Bruno Bettelheim, "Joey: A 'Mechanical Boy'"	___	___	___
Sissela Bok, "To Lie or Not to Lie? — The Doctor's Dilemma"	___	___	___
Jorge Luis Borges, "The Gaucho and the City: Stories of Horsemen"	___	___	___
Joan Didion, "On Keeping a Notebook"	___	___	___
Nora Ephron, "A Few Words about Breasts: Shaping Up Absurd"	___	___	___
Robert Finch, "Very Like a Whale"	___	___	___
Paul Goodman, "A Proposal to Abolish Grading"	___	___	___
Elizabeth Janeway, "Soaps, Cynicism, and Mind Control"	___	___	___
X. J. Kennedy, "Who Killed King Kong?"	___	___	___
C. S. Lewis, "The Trouble with 'X' . . ."	___	___	___
Flannery O'Connor, "Total Effect and the Eighth Grade"	___	___	___
George Orwell, "Politics and the English Language"	___	___	___
Studs Terkel, "Fathers and Sons"	___	___	___

To the Student

Please help us make *Barnet & Stubbs's Practical Guide to Writing, With Additional Readings,* an even better book. To improve our textbooks, we revise them every few years, taking into account the experiences of both instructors and students with the previous editions. At some time, your instructor will most likely be asked to comment extensively on *Barnet & Stubbs's Practical Guide to Writing, With Additional Readings.* Now we would like to hear from you.

Complete this questionnaire and return it to:

College English Developmental Group
Little, Brown and Company
34 Beacon St.
Boston, MA 02106

School _____

City, State, Zip Code _____

Course title _____

Instructor's full name _____

Other books required _____

_____

1. Did you like the book? _____

2. Was it too easy? _____Too difficult? _____

   Did you read it all? _____

   Which chapters were most useful? Why? _____

   _____

   _____

   Which chapters were least useful? Why? _____

   _____

   _____

guilty of vices ("You should not molest children") unless the essay is clearly aimed at an audience that admits to these vices, say a pamphlet directed to child molesters who are seeking help. Thus, it is acceptable to say, "If you are a poor speller," but it is not acceptable to say, to the general reader, "You should improve your spelling"; the reader's spelling may not need improvement. And avoid *you* when the word cannot possibly apply to the reader: "A hundred years ago you were faced with many diseases that now have been eradicated." Something like "A hundred years ago people were faced . . ." is preferable.

your, you're The first is a possessive pronoun ("your book"); the second is a contraction of *you are* ("You're mistaken").

LAST WORDS

A rich patron once gave money to the painter Chu Ta, asking him to paint a picture of a fish. Three years later, when he still had not received the painting, the patron went to Chu Ta's house to ask why the picture was not done. Chu Ta did not answer, but dipped a brush in ink and with a few strokes drew a splendid fish. "If it is so easy," asked the patron, "why didn't you give me the picture three years ago?" Again Chu Ta did not answer. Instead, he opened the door of a large cabinet. Thousands of pictures of fish tumbled out.

AUTHOR BIOGRAPHIES

Maya Angelou was born in St. Louis in 1928. Among her writings are two books of poetry and three autobiographical books. "Graduation" (editors' title) is from the first autobiographical volume, *I Know Why the Caged Bird Sings*.

Russell Baker, born in Virginia in 1925, has been a professional journalist since 1947, when he joined the *Baltimore Sun*. Later he covered Washington for *The New York Times,* and he now writes a widely syndicated column, "The Observer." "The Flag" was originally published in this column, and reprinted in a collection of his essays entitled *So This Is Depravity* (1980). "Coming to Grips with Death" is from *Growing Up,* an autobiography that won the 1982 Pulitzer Prize for biography. The title of the selection is ours.

James Baldwin was born in Harlem in 1924, and graduated from De Witt Clinton High School. At first he did odd jobs while he wrote, but in 1948 he received a fellowship that enabled him to go to Paris, where he wrote two novels (*Go Tell It on the Mountain* and *Giovanni's Room*), as well as essays published in *Notes of a Native Son*. He returned to the United States in 1955, where he has continued to publish fiction, plays, and essays.

Robert Benchley (1889–1945) was educated at Harvard, where, he said, he learned that one cannot attend two courses at the same hour, and that one can wear a sock with a hole in the toe if one turns the sock inside out. Benchley wrote humorous essays and performed on radio and in films.

Bruno Bettelheim was born in Vienna in 1903. He came to the United States in 1939, and became a naturalized citizen in 1944. From 1943 to 1973 he was head of the Sonia Shankman Orthogenic School in Chicago, where he also taught psychology at the University of Chicago. He is now retired, but continues to write on psychology.

Black Elk, a *wichasha wakon* (holy man) of the Oglala Sioux, as a small boy witnessed the Battle of Little Bighorn (1876). He lived to see his people all but annihilated and his hopes for them extinguished. In 1931, toward the end of his life, he told his life story to the poet and scholar John G. Neihardt in order to preserve a sacred vision given him. "High Horse's Courting" provides a comic interlude in a predominantly tragic memoir.

Sissela Bok teaches courses in medical ethics and in decision-making at the Harvard Medical School. She is the author of *Lying*, a book concerned with such problems as whether or not to lie to people for their own good.

Jorge Luis Borges was born in Argentina in 1899. Poet, essayist, story writer, and teacher, he is widely regarded as the greatest living man of letters writing in Spanish.

J. Bronowski (1908–1974) was born in Poland and was educated in England. Trained as a mathematician, Bronowski distinguished himself as a writer not only about science but also about literature and psychology.

Leonard Cammer (1914–1978), a specialist in the treatment of severe depression and schizophrenia, taught and practiced psychiatry in New York City.

Bruce Catton (1899–1978), after serving as a reporter for several newspapers, turned much of his attention to studying the Civil War, but he continued to work in journalism, for example by serving as Director of Information for the United States Department of Commerce. His historical writing won him a Pulitzer Prize and a National Book Award.

Joan Didion was born in California in 1934 and educated at the University of California, Berkeley. While she was still a senior she wrote a prize-winning essay for a contest sponsored by *Vogue*, and soon she became an associate feature editor for *Vogue*. She has written novels, essays, and screenplays.

Jim Doherty, a writer and editor, served as executive editor for *National Wildlife*.

Nora Ephron, born in 1941, is the daughter of two Hollywood writers. She has published several volumes of essays.

Bergen Evans (1904–1978) taught English at Northwestern University for many years, and achieved national prominence as the moderator of several television programs and as the author of *The Natural History of Nonsense* and other books.

Robert Finch is publications director of the Cape Cod Museum of Natural History and a member of the Breadloaf Writers' Conference at Middlebury College. This essay is from his first book, *Common Ground: A Naturalist's Cape Cod* (1981).

E[dward] M[organ] Forster (1879–1970) was born in London and was graduated from King's College, Cambridge. He traveled widely and lived for

a while in India, but most of his life was spent back at King's College. His best-known novel is *A Passage to India* (1926).

Paul Goodman (1911–1972) received his bachelor's degree from City College in New York, and his Ph.D. from the University of Chicago. He taught in several colleges and universities, and wrote prolifically on literature, politics, and education.

Jeff Greenfield has written speeches for Robert F. Kennedy and John V. Lindsay, and has exchanged sharp words with William F. Buckley on television. He has published essays on sports and on other popular entertainments.

Jane Jacobs was born in Scranton, Pennsylvania, in 1916. From 1952 until 1962 she served as an associate editor of *Architectural Forum*. In addition to writing *The Death and Life of Great American Cities*, from which our selection comes, she has written *The Economy of Cities*.

Elizabeth Janeway was born in Brooklyn and educated at Swarthmore and Barnard. A novelist, critic, and lecturer, she is especially concerned with the social context that has produced the women's movement.

Susan Jacoby has worked as a reporter for the *Washington Post* and as a columnist for *The New York Times*.

X. J. Kennedy was born in 1929 in New Jersey. He has published several books of poetry (including a book for children) and several textbooks.

Martin Luther King (1929–1968), clergyman and civil rights leader, achieved national fame in 1955–56 when he led the boycott against segregated bus lines in Montgomery, Alabama. In 1964 he was awarded the Nobel Peace Prize, but he continued to encounter strong opposition. On 4 April 1968, while in Memphis to support striking sanitation workers, he was shot and killed.

Edward Koch, born in 1924 in New York City, was educated at City College and at New York University Law School. Long active in Democratic politics, Mr. Koch has served as mayor of New York since 1978.

Jonathan Kozol, born in 1936, has taught in elementary schools in Massachusetts. The author of several books, he is best known for *Death at an Early Age: The Destruction of the Hearts and Minds of Negro Children in the Boston Public Schools.*

Chuck Kraemer was born in 1945 in Marysville, Kansas. He received a bachelor's degree from the University of Kansas and did graduate work

in film at Boston University. He has written essays, chiefly on film, for *The New York Times* and for other newspapers.

Barbara Lawrence was born in Hanover, New Hampshire, and was educated at Connecticut College and at New York University. She teaches at the State University of New York, at Old Westbury.

C[live] S[taples] Lewis (1898–1963) taught medieval and Renaissance literature at Oxford and later at Cambridge. In addition to writing about literature, he wrote fiction (including children's books), poetry, and numerous essays and books on moral and religious topics.

Alan Lightman was born in Memphis in 1948, and educated at Princeton and California Institute of Technology. A theoretical astrophysicist who teaches at Harvard, for this essay, published in *The New York Times Magazine,* he looked inward rather than upward.

Malcolm X, born Malcolm Little in Nebraska in 1925, was the son of a Baptist minister. He completed the eighth grade but then got into trouble and was sent to a reformatory. After his release he became a thief, dope peddler, and pimp; in 1944 he was sent to jail, where he spent six and a half years. During his years in jail he became a convert to the Black Muslim faith. Paroled in 1950, he served as a minister and founded Muslim temples throughout the United States. In 1964, however, he broke with Elijah Muhammad, leader of the Black Muslims, and formed a new group, the Organization of Afro-American Unity. The next year he was assassinated in New York.

Anne Hebald Mandelbaum was born in New York City in 1944, and was educated at Radcliffe College and Yale University. She is a free-lance writer.

Margaret Mead (1901–1978) was born in Philadelphia and educated at De Pauw University, Barnard College, and Columbia University. She lived in Samoa in 1925 and 1926; in 1928 she published the book that promptly established her reputation, *Coming of Age in Samoa.* Throughout the next fifty years she wrote prolifically and lectured widely on sociological and anthropological subjects.

Rhoda Metraux was born in Brooklyn in 1914. An anthropologist who has done field work in many parts of the world, she is a research associate of the American Museum of Natural History.

Jonathan Miller, an Englishman born in 1934, is widely known as a writer, actor, and director of plays, operas, and television programs. But he is also a physician and a student of the history of medicine. His medical

background enabled him to write and direct a series of television programs entitled *The Body in Question.*

Flannery O'Connor (1925–1964) was born in Georgia and spent most of her short life there. *The Complete Stories of Flannery O'Connor* received the National Book Award for fiction in 1971; another posthumous volume, *Mystery and Manners*, includes essays on literature and an account of her experiences raising peacocks in Georgia.

George Orwell (1903–1950), an Englishman, adopted this name; he was born Eric Blair, in India. He was educated at Eton, in England, but in 1921 he returned to the East and served for five years as a police officer in Burma. He then returned to Europe, doing odd jobs while writing novels and stories. In 1936 he fought in the Spanish Civil War on the side of the Republicans, an experience reported in *Homage to Catalonia* (1938). His last years were spent writing in England.

Noel Perrin, born in New York in 1927, farms in Vermont and teaches American literature at Dartmouth College. Among his publications are three books of essays, chiefly on rural subjects.

Robert M. Pirsig, born in Minneapolis in 1928, has published one book, *Zen and the Art of Motorcycle Maintenance,* a narrative of a motorcycle trip taken by a father and his eleven-year-old, who travel from Minneapolis to the Pacific. As our extract on "Mechanic's Feel" suggests, the book is highly meditative, in large part an account of complex relationships with our environment.

Sylvia Plath (1932–1963), educated at Smith College, is known chiefly as a poet, but she also wrote fiction, letters, and a journal.

Philip Roth was born in Newark, New Jersey, in 1933. His first book, *Goodbye, Columbus,* won a National Book Award for fiction. Among his other notable books are *Letting Go, Portnoy's Complaint,* and *Reading Myself and Others.*

Nancy Masterson Sakamoto, professor of Buddhism at the University of Hawaii, lived for a while in Osaka, where she taught English to Japanese people. The essay we print is a chapter from a textbook written in English, used by Japanese students taking a course in conversational English.

Sei Shōnagon was born about 965 in Japan; for some ten years she served as lady-in-waiting to the Empress Sadako. The tradition that she died poor and alone may be true, or it may be the moralists' attempt to reply to her sensual life.

Max Shulman, born in St. Paul in 1919, is the author of many humorous books and of the television series *Dobie Gillis.*

Christopher D. Stone was born in 1937 in New York City. He holds a law degree from Yale, and teaches law at the University of Southern California.

I[sidore] F[einstein] Stone, born in Philadelphia in 1907, was educated at the University of Pennsylvania. For some twenty years he worked as a reporter and edited a leftist newsletter, *I. F. Stone's Bi-weekly,* noted for its incisive criticism of American politics. He now occasionally publishes in *The New York Review of Books.*

Studs Terkel was born Louis Terkel in New York City in 1912. He was brought up in Chicago and was graduated from the University of Chicago. Terkel has been an actor, playwright, columnist, and disc jockey, but he is best known as the man who makes books out of tape recordings of people he gets to talk. These oral histories are *Division Street: America* (1966), *Hard Times* (1970), *Working* (1974), and *American Dreams: Lost and Found* (1980). In 1978 Terkel published his memoirs, *Talking to Myself.*

Paul Theroux was born in 1941 in Medford, Massachusetts, and was educated at the University of Maine, the University of Massachusetts, and Syracuse University. He served as a Peace Corps volunteer in Africa, and has spent much of his adult life abroad, in Africa, Asia, Europe, and Central America. Though best known as a novelist and writer of travel books, he is also a poet and essayist. This essay originally appeared in *The New York Times Magazine.*

Lewis Thomas was born in 1913. A distinguished medical researcher and administrator, he is president of the Memorial Sloan-Kettering Cancer Center in New York. He is also a writer; he has published *Lives of a Cell,* a collection of twenty-nine short essays, which won a National Book Award in 1974, and *The Medusa and the Snail.*

Henry David Thoreau (1817–1862), naturalist, social and political activist, and (of course) writer, in 1845 went to live for a while at Walden Pond in Massachusetts, where he hoped to be free enough from distractions to study life closely, or, as he put it, "to drive life into a corner, . . . to know it by experience, and be able to give a true account of it."

Lester Thurow was born in Montana and educated at Williams College, Balliol College, and Harvard. A professor of economics at MIT, he is the author of books and articles not only for specialists but also for the general reader. This essay appeared in *The New York Times,* 8 March 1981.

John Updike was born in Shillington, Pennsylvania, in 1932. He has published stories, novels, and essays. In 1963, *The Centaur,* a novel, received a National Book Award.

E[lwyn] B[rooks] White wrote poetry and fiction, but he is most widely known as an essayist and as the coauthor (with William Strunk) of *Elements of Style.* After a long career at *The New Yorker* he retired to Maine, but he continued to write until the year before his death at the age of 86.

Virginia Woolf (1882–1941) was born in London into an upper-middle class literary family. In 1912 she married a writer, and with him she founded The Hogarth Press, whose important publications included not only books by T. S. Eliot but her own novels.

(Continued from page iv)

Russell Baker, "The Flag." Reprinted by permission of Don Congdon Associates, Inc. Copyright © 1975 by Russell Baker.

James Baldwin, "Stranger in the Village." From *Notes of a Native Son* by James Baldwin. Copyright © 1955 by James Baldwin. Reprinted by permission of Beacon Press.

Pat Bellanca, "Jimmy Buffett is Going Coconuts" from *The Wellesley News*, 13 March 1981. Reprinted by permission of the author.

Saul Bellow, excerpt reprinted from *The Victim* by Saul Bellow by permission of the publisher, Vanguard Press, Inc. Copyright 1947 by Saul Bellow. Copyright renewed 1974 by Saul Bellow.

Robert Benchley, "How to Get Things Done" by Robert Benchley from *The Benchley Roundup*, selected by Nathaniel Benchley. Copyright, 1930 by Chicago Tribune/New York News Syndicate, Inc. By permission of Harper & Row, Publishers, Inc.

Bruno Bettelheim, "Joey: A Mechanical Boy," *Scientific American*, March 1959. Reprinted with permission; copyright © 1959 by Scientific American, Inc. All rights reserved.

Robert Bly, "Love Poem" from *Silence in the Snowy Fields* (Middletown, Conn.: Wesleyan University Press, 1962). Copyright © 1962 by Robert Bly. Reprinted by permission of the author.

Sissela Bok, "To Lie or Not to Lie? — The Doctor's Dilemma," *The New York Times*, 18 April, 1978. Copyright © 1978 by The New York Times Company. Reprinted by permission.

Jose Luis Borges, "The Gaucho and the City: Stories of Horsemen," *The New Republic*, May 19, 1982. Reprinted by permission of *The New Republic*, © 1982 The New Republic, Inc.

Jacob Bronowski, "The Reach of Imagination." From *A Sense of the Future* (Cambridge, Mass.: MIT Press, 1977), pp. 21–31. Originally in *Proceedings of the American Academy of Arts and Letters and the National Institute of Arts and Letters* (1967), 2d series II, and reprinted with their permission.

Anthony Burgess, excerpt from *Language Made Plain*. Copyright © 1964 by Anthony Burgess. Reprinted by permission.

Leonard Cammer, "How to Deal with the Crying," from *Up from Depression*. Copyright © 1969 by Leonard Cammer, M.D. Reprinted by permission of Simon & Schuster, Inc.

Bruce Catton, "Grant and Lee: A Study in Contrasts" from *The American Story*, Earl Schenck Miers, editor. © 1956 by Broadcast Music, Inc. Copyright renewed 1984. Reprinted by permission.

Confidential Chat, a feature of *The Boston Globe*. Letters by Three Begonias and The First Waffle used by permission.

Sharon Curtin, excerpts from *Nobody Ever Died of Old Age* by Sharon Curtin. Copyright © 1972 by Sharon Curtin. By permission of Little, Brown and Company in association with the Atlantic Monthly Press.

Joan Didion, "Los Angeles Notebook." Reprinted by permission of Farrar, Straus and Giroux, Inc. from *Slouching Towards Bethlehem* by Joan Didion. Copyright © 1967, 1968 by Joan Didion.

Joan Didion, "On Keeping a Notebook." Reprinted by permission of Farrar, Straus & Giroux, Inc. from *Slouching Towards Bethlehem* by Joan Didion. Copyright © 19 , 1968 by Joan Didion.

Paul Diederich, from *Measuring Growth In English*, pp. 21–22. Copyright © 1974 National Council of Teachers of English. Reprinted by permission of the publisher.

Jim Doherty, "How Cemeteries Bring Us Back to Earth," *The New York Times*, 31 May 1982. Copyright © 1982 by The New York Times Company. Reprinted by permission.

Mamie Duff, "Dedication Doth Not a Good Teacher Make." Reprinted by permission of Mamie Duff, Staff, Lockwood Press.

Nora Ephron, "A Few Words about Breasts: Shaping Up Absurd." From *Crazy Salad: Some Things About Women*, by Nora Ephron. Copyright © 1972 by Nora Ephron. Reprinted by permission of Alfred A. Knopf, Inc.

Bergen Evans, "Sophistication," *The New York Times Book Review*, 7 September 1971. Copyright © 1971 by The New York Times Company. Reprinted by permission.

Robert Finch, "Very Like a Whale." From *Common Ground: A Naturalist's Cape Cod* by Robert Finch. Copyright © 1981 by Robert Finch. Reprinted by permission of David R. Godine, Publisher, Boston.

E. M. Forster, "My Wood" from *Abinger Harvest*, copyright 1936, 1964 by E. M. Forster. Reprinted by permission of Harcourt Brace Jovanovich, Inc. and Edward Arnold (Publishers) Ltd.

Patricia Freeman, "The Einstein of Happiness," *California Living*, 23 October 1983. Reprinted by permission.

Eileen Garred, "Ethnobotanists Race Against Time to Save Useful Plants," *Harvard University Gazette*, 24 May 1985. Reprinted by permission of the *Harvard University Gazette*.

Margaret Gooch, library exercises (following research paper in Chapter 10) reprinted by permission of Margaret Gooch, Wessell Library, Tufts University.

Paul Goodman, "A Proposal to Abolish Grading" (editors' title). Reprinted from *Compulsory Mis-Education* by Paul Goodman, copyright 1964, by permission of the publisher, Horizon Press, New York.

Jeff Greenfield, "Columbo Knows the Butler Didn't Do It," *The New York Times*, 22 April 1973. Copyright © 1973 by The New York Times Company. Reprinted by permission.

"In Search of the Elusive Pingo" (Ideas and Trends), *The New York Times*, 5 May 1974. Copyright © 1974 by The New York Times Company. Reprinted by permission.

Jane Jacobs, "The Use of Sidewalks" (original title, "The Uses of Sidewalk Safety") from *The Death and Life of Great American Cities*, by Jane Jacobs. Copyright © 1961 by Jane Jacobs. Reprinted by permission of Random House, Inc.

Susan Jacoby, "Too Many Women Are Misconstruing Feminism's Nature," *The New York Times*, 14 April 1983. Reprinted by permission of the author. Copyright © 1983 by Susan Jacoby.

Elizabeth Janeway, "Soaps, Cynicism, and Mind Control," *Ms.* Magazine, January 1985. Reprinted by permission of the author.

James Weldon Johnson, lines from "Lift Ev'ry Voice and Sing," © Copyright: Edward B. Marks Music Corporation. Reprinted by permission.

George Kane, "Traveler's Diarist," *The New Republic*, 14 March 1981. © 1981 The New Republic, Inc. Reprinted by permission.

X. J. Kennedy, "Who Killed King Kong?" *Dissent* Magazine, Spring 1960. Reprinted by permission of the publisher and author.

Martin Luther King, Jr., "Nonviolent Resistance," (editors' title). From pp. 211–216 in *Stride Toward Freedom* by Martin Luther King, Jr. Copyright © 1958 by Martin Luther King, Jr. By permission of Harper and Row, Publishers, Inc.

Carole Klein, "The Tough Got Going," *The New York Times Book Review*, 17 February 1985. Copyright © 1985 by The New York Times Company. Reprinted by permission.

Edward I. Koch, "Death and Justice: How Capital Punishment Affirms Life," *The New Republic*, April 15, 1985. Reprinted by permission of *The New Republic*. © 1985 The New Republic, Inc.

Jonathan Kozol, "Operation Illiteracy," *The New York Times*, 5 March 1979. Copyright © 1979 by The New York Times Company. Reprinted by permission.

Chuck Kraemer, "Indecent Exposure," *The Real Paper*, 4 June 1975. Reprinted by permission of *The Real Paper*.

Barbara Lawrence, "Four Letter Words Can Hurt You," (original title, "—— Isn't a Dirty Word"), *The New York Times*, 27 October 1973. Copyright © 1973 by The New York Times Company. Reprinted by permission.

"Letter to the Editor" by Leonard S. Charlap, *The New York Times*, 19 December 1977. Copyright © 1977 by The New York Times Company. Reprinted by permission.

"Letter to the Editor" by Ruth H. Cohn, *The New York Times*, 20 July 1978. Copyright © 1978 by The New York Times Company. Reprinted by permission.

C. S. Lewis, "The Trouble with X" from *God in the Dock*, edited by Walter Hooper (British title, *Undeceptions*). Copyright © 1970, 1971 by the Trustees of the Estate of C. S. Lewis. Reprinted by permission of Curtis Brown Ltd. and William Collins Sons & Co. Ltd.

C. S. Lewis, "Vivisection" from *God in the Dock*, edited by Walter Hooper (British title, *Undeceptions*). Copyright © 1970, 1971 by the Trustees of the Estate of C. S. Lewis. Reprinted by permission of Curtis Brown Ltd. and William Collins Sons & Co. Ltd.

Alan P. Lightman, "Elapsed Expectations," *The New York Times Magazine*, 25 March 1984. Copyright © 1984 by The New York Times Company. Reprinted by permission.

Walter Lippmann, excerpt from column in *The New York Times*, 20 February 1942. Copyright © 1942 by The New York Times Company. Reprinted by permission.

K. N. Llewellyn, excerpt reprinted with permission from Llewellyn, K. N., *The Bramble Bush: On Law and Its Study* (Oceana Publications, Inc., 1981).

Malcolm X, "Rejected" (editors' title) from *The Autobiography of Malcolm X*, by Malcolm X., with the assistance of Alex Haley. Copyright © 1964 by Alex Haley and Malcolm X. Copyright © 1965 by Alex Haley and Betty Shabazz. Reprinted by permission of Random House, Inc.

Anne Hebald Mandelbaum, "It's the Portly Penguin That Gets the Girl, French Biologist Claims," *Harvard University Gazette*, 30 January 1976. Reprinted by permission of the *Harvard University Gazette*.

Jack Margolis, "And All Those Others" from *The Poetry of Richard Milhous Nixon* (Los Angeles: Cliff House Books, 1974). Reprinted by permission of the author and publisher.

Sister Lydia Martin-Boyle, H.O.O.M., "Adman's Atlanta." Reprinted by permission of the author.

Gerald Mast, excerpts from *The Comic Mind*, pp. 281–283. Copyright © 1973 by Gerald Mast. Reprinted by permission of the Bobbs-Merrill Co., Inc.

Margaret Mead and Rhoda Metraux, "On Friendship — August 1966" from *A Way of Seeing* (1970) by Margaret Mead and Rhoda Metraux. Copyright © 1966 by Margaret Mead and Rhoda Metraux. By permission of William Morrow & Company.

Jonathan Miller, from *The Body In Question*, by Jonathan Miller. Copyright © 1978 by Jonathan Miller. Reprinted by permission of Random House, Inc. and Jonathan Cape Ltd.

Anne Moody, excerpt from *Coming of Age in Mississippi* by Anne Moody. Copyright © 1968 by Anne Moody. Reprinted by permission of Doubleday & Company, Inc.

Joseph Morgenstern, excerpt from "On the Road," *Newsweek*, 21 July 1969. Copyright 1969, by Newsweek, Inc. All Rights Reserved. Reprinted by permission.

John G. Neihardt, "High Horse's Courting" from *Black Elk Speaks* by John G. Neihardt, copyright 1959, 1961; courtesy John G. Neihardt Trust.

"Notes and Comment," *The New Yorker*, 10 January 1970. Reprinted by permission; © 1970 The New Yorker Magazine, Inc.

"Notes and Comment," *The New Yorker*, 22 September 1975. Reprinted by permission; © 1975 The New Yorker Magazine, Inc.

Flannery O'Connor, "Total Effect and the Eighth Grade," from *Mystery and Manners* by Flannery O'Connor, ed. by Sally and Robert Fitzgerald, pp. 135–140. Copyright © 1957, 1961, 1963, 1964, 1966, 1967, 1969 by the Estate of Mary Flannery O'Connor. Copyright © 1962 by Flannery O'Connor. Reprinted by permission of Farrar, Straus and Giroux, Inc.

George Orwell, excerpt from "England Your England" from *The Collected Essays, Journalism, and Letters of George Orwell*, Vol. II, Angus Ian and Sonia Orwell, eds., 1968. Reprinted by permission of Harcourt Brace Jovanovich, Inc., the estate of the late Sonia Brownell Orwell, and Martin Secker & Warburg Ltd.

George Orwell, "Politics and the English Language" from *Shooting an Elephant and Other Essays*. Copyright 1950 by Sonia Brownell Orwell; renewed 1978 by Sonia Pitt-Rivers. Reprinted by permission of Harcourt Brace Jovanovich, Inc., the estate of the late Sonia Brownell Orwell, and Martin Secker & Warburg Ltd.

George Orwell, "Shooting an Elephant" from *Shooting an Elephant and Other Essays*. Copyright 1945, 1946, 1949, 1950, by Sonia Brownell Orwell; renewed 1978 by Sonia Pitt-Rivers. Reprinted by permission of Harcourt Brace Jovanovich, Inc., the estate of the late Sonia Brownell Orwell, and Martin Secker & Warburg Ltd.

Dorothy Parker, "News Item" from *The Portable Dorothy Parker*. Revised and enlarged edition. Copyright 1936, copyright © renewed 1964 by Dorothy Parker. Reprinted by permission of Viking Penguin Inc.

Noel Perrin, "The Androgynous Man," *The New York Times Magazine*, 5 February 1984. Copyright © 1984 by The New York Times Company. Reprinted by permission.

Marge Piercy, lines from "Rough Times" from *Living in the Open* by Marge Piercy. Copyright © 1972, 1976 by Marge Piercy. Reprinted by permission of Alfred A. Knopf, Inc.

Robert M. Pirsig, excerpts from p. 14 and pp. 323–4 in *Zen and the Art of Motorcycle Maintenance* by Robert M. Pirsig. Copyright © 1974 by Robert M. Pirsig. By permission of William Morrow and Company.

Sylvia Plath, from *The Journals of Sylvia Plath*, edited by Frances McCullough. Copyright © 1982 by Ted Hughes as Executor of the estate of Sylvia Plath. Additional text copyright © 1982 by Frances McCullough. Reprinted by permission of The Dial Press.

Susan Pope, "Tennis Tips to a Beginner." Reprinted by permission of the author.

Charles T. Powers, "Say One Word and I'll Cut Your Throat," *Los Angeles Times*, 13 January 1974. Copyright, 1974, Los Angeles Times. Reprinted by permission.

Random House Dictionary of the English Language definition of *feminism*. Copyright © 1966 by Random House, Inc. Reprinted by permission.

Reuters, "Fish Eat Brazilian Fisherman," *The Boston Globe*, 17 January 1971. Reprinted by permission of Reuters.

Philip Roth, "The Newark Public Library" (original title, "Topics: Reflections on the Death of a Library"), *The New York Times*, 1 March 1969. Copyright © 1969 by The New York Times Company. Reprinted by permission.

David Royce, excerpt from "Moby Balloon," *The New York Times Magazine*, 26 May 1974. Copyright © 1974 by The New York Times Company. Reprinted by permission.

Nancy Sakamoto, "Conversational Ballgames" from *Polite Fictions* (Tokyo: Kinseido Ltd., 1982). Reprinted by permission of Kinseido Ltd.

Sei Shōnagon, "The Pillow Book of Sei Shonagon" from *The Pillow Book of Sei Shōnagon*, translated and edited by Ivan Morris (1967). Reprinted by permission of Columbia University Press and Oxford University Press.

Max Shulman, "Love is a Fallacy." Copyright 1951, © renewed 1979 by Max Shulman. Reprinted by permission of Harold Matson Company.

Gary Snyder, "Hitch Haiku" from *The Back Country* by Gary Snyder. Copyright © 1968 by Gary Snyder. Reprinted by permission of New Directions Publishing Corporation.

Virginia Woolf, "Professions for Women" from *The Death of the Moth and Other Essays* by Virginia Woolf. Copyright 1942 by Harcourt Brace Jovanovich; copyright 1970 by Marjorie T. Powers, executrix. Reprinted by permission of Harcourt Brace Jovanovich, Inc. and The Hogarth Press Ltd.

William Butler Yeats, lines from "The Balloon of the Mind" reprinted with permission of Macmillan Publishing Company. Michael B. Yeats, and Macmillan London from *Collected Poems* by W. B. Yeats. Copyright 1919 by Macmillan Publishing Company, renewed 1947 by Bertha Georgie Yeats.

William Butler Yeats, lines from "The friends that have it I do wrong" reprinted with permission of Macmillan Publishing Company, Michael B. Yeats, and Macmillan London from *The Variorum Edition of the Poems of W. B. Yeats*, edited by Peter Allt and Russell K. Alspach (New York: Macmillan, 1957).

Art

Pieter Brueghel, *The Painter and the Connoisseur.* Graphische Sammlung Albertina, Wien.

Shaka nyorai. Japanese, Heian Period. Late 10th century. Single wood-block construction, painted and gilded. H 82.5 cm. Denman Waldo Ross Collection. 09.72. Courtesy, Museum of Fine Arts, Boston.

Bodhisattva Kuan Yin Seated in Royal Ease Position. Chinese, Sung dynasty. Carved wood, decorated in gold, lacquer, and polychrome. Reportedly from Chishan, Shansi province. H 1.41 m × W .88 m × D .88 m. Harvey Edward Wetzel Fund. 20.590. Courtesy, Museum of Fine Arts, Boston.

William Notman, Sitting Bull, and Buffalo Bill. Courtesy, Notman Photographic Archives, McCord Museum, McGill University.

Woman Holding Up Her Dying Lover. Francisco de Goya y Lucientes. Spanish, 1746–1828. Brush and gray wash, touched with brown wash. 9¼ × 5¹¹⁄₁₆ in. (234 × 145 mm). Gift of Frederick J. Kennedy Memorial Foundation. 1973. 700b. Courtesy, Museum of Fine Arts, Boston.

Francisco de Goya y Lucientes, *El amor y la muerte.* Courtesy, Museo del Prado, Madrid.

Covered Car — Long Beach, California. Copyright, Robert Frank, from *The Americans*, 1958.

Westchester, New York, Farm House. Courtesy, John T. Hill, Executor, Estate of Walker Evans.

Leonardo da Vinci, Mona Lisa. Alinari/Art Resource, New York.

"Spaghetti," from MAZES II by Vladimir Koziakin. Copyright 1972 by Vladimir Koziakin. Reprinted by permission of the Berkley Publishing Group.

"Atlanta" advertisement reprinted by permission of Atlanta Chamber of Commerce.

Index

a/an, 719
abbreviations, 704
above, 719
academics, 719
accept/except, 719
active voice, 469–71
adjectives in series, 692–93
"Adman's Atlanta," 259
adverb, conjunctive, 687, 690
affect/effect, 719
aggravate, 719
agreement
  noun and pronoun, 479
  subject and verb, 480
Alexander, Jacob
  "Nitrites: Cancer for Many,
    Money for Few," 357
all ready/already, 719
all right/alright, 719
all together/altogether, 719
allusion/illusion, 720
almost/most, 731
a lot/alot, 720
already/all ready, 719
alright/all right, 719
altogether/all together, 719
ambiguity, 476, 478–79
among/between, 722–23
amount/number, 720
an/a, 719
analogy, 199–200, 460–62
analysis, 35–55, 250–52
analyzation/analysis, 720

"And All Those Others," 537
and etc., 626
and/or, 626
"Androgynous Man, The," 146
Angelou, Maya
  "Graduation," 286
Anonymous
  "Eclipse," 265
  letter on rape, 273
ante/anti, 720
anthology/collection, 720
anti/ante, 720
anticlimax, 491–92
anxious, 720
anybody/any body, 721
anyone/any one, 721
apostrophe, 702–03
application, letter of, 425–26
apposition, appositive, 691
area of, 721
argument, 188–204
  organization of, 203–04
argumentum ad hominem, 199
around, 721
as/like, 721
as of now, 722
aspect, 722
as such, 722
as to, 722
assumptions, 200–01
audience, 15–18, 28, 392,
  410
authority, false, 195–96

bad/badly, 722
Baker, Russell
  "Coming to Grips with Death,"
    303
  "The Flag," 555
Baldwin, James
  "Stranger in the Village," 560
"Balloon of the Mind, The," 1,
    389
"Battle of the Ants, The," 654
because/since, 736
"Beer Can," 521
begging the question, 198–99
being, 722
being that/being so, 722
Bellanca, Pat
  "Jimmy Buffett Is Going
    Coconuts?!" 396
Bellow, Saul, 253
Benchley, Robert
  "How to Get Things Done,"
    572
Benjamin Franklin's exercise, 531–
    32
beside/besides, 722
Bettelheim, Bruno
  "Joey: A 'Mechanical Boy,'"
    577
between/among, 722–23
"Beyond the Institution: The
    Effects of Labeling on Ex-
    Mental Patients," 373
biannually/semiannually, 723
Bible, references to, 677
bibliographic notes, 321–22, 323
bibliography, 318, 342–54
bimonthly/semimonthly, 723
biweekly/semiweekly, 723
Black/black, 723
Black Elk
  "High Horse's Courting," 297

Bly, Robert
  "Love Poem," 485
"Body in Question, The," 177
Bok, Sissela
  "To Lie or Not to Lie? — The
    Doctor's Dilemma," 586
book review(s)
  indexes to, 316–17
  references to, 351
  writing a, 391–95
Borges, Jorge Luis
  "The Gaucho and the City:
    Stories of Horsemen," 588
brackets, 674–75
Bronowski, Jacob
  "The Reach of Imagination,"
    138

Cammer, Leonard
  "How to Deal with the
    Crying," 159
can/may, 723
capital letters, 699–700
card catalog, 312–15
cats are dogs, 473–74
Catton, Bruce
  "Grant and Lee: A Study in
    Contrasts," 70
cause and effect, 163
centers on/centers around, 723
choppiness, 492–95
circular reasoning, 198–99
circumlocutions, 437–38
clarity, 18–20, 450–89, 529–30
classification, 37–43
clauses
  cutting, 444–47
  dependent (subordinate), 497
  extra, 444–47
  independent (main), 497
  introductory, 689

who, which, that, 445–46
clichés, 464–65, 466–67
coherence
in paragraphs, 94–97
in sentences, 472–82
collection/anthology, 720
collective nouns, 723
colon, 685–86
"Columbo Knows the Butler
Didn't Do It," 64
"Coming to Grips with Death,"
303
comma, 688–94
as parentheses, 690
with a series, 692–93
with direct discourse, 693
with independent clauses, 689
with introductory material, 689
with nonrestrictive modifiers,
691–92
with tacked on material, 689–
90
position with other punctuation,
694–95
comma fault, 682–84
comma splice, 682–84
common knowledge, 328–29
compare/contrast, 723
comparison, 45–52
complement/compliment, 723
complex sentence, 497
compliment/complement, 723
compound-complex sentence, 497
compound sentence, 497
comprise, 723–24
computers, 383–86, 716
"Conceit," 493
concept, 724
conciseness, 431–49
concluding paragraphs, 109–13
conclusions, empty, 440

concrete (specific) details, 18–20,
188–89, 457–58
conjunctions
coordinating, 497, 682, 689
subordinating, 681–82, 683
conjunctive adverb, 687, 690
connotation, 454–56
contact, 724
continual/continuous, 724
contractions, 703
contrast/compare, 723
"Conversational Ballgames," 180
coordinating conjunction, 497,
682, 689
corrections in manuscript, 670–72
could have/could of, 732
criteria/criterion, 724
cumulative sentence, 534–36

dangling modifiers, 476–77
dash, 694–95
data/datum, 724
dates, 705
"Dave Stribling," 647
"Death and Justice: How Capital
Punishment Affirms Life,"
237
"Dedication Doth Not a Good
Teacher Make," 22
deduction, 201–03
definitely, 437
definition, 118–29
deletions, 671
denotation, 453–54
dependent clause, 497
description, 243–52
details, 18–20
dictionary, 118–19n
Didion, Joan
"Los Angeles Notebook," 262
"On Keeping a Notebook," 592

different from/different than, 724
dilemma, 724
disinterested/uninterested, 724
documentation, 333–56
"Dodgers Keep Perfect Record in
    Knocking Out Southpaws,"
    462
Doherty, Jim
    "How Cemeteries Bring Us
    Back to Earth," 250
Donne, John
    "The Flea," 210
"Door, The," 661
Doyle, Arthur Conan
    "The Science of Deduction," 52
draft, 5–7, 26–28, 330–32
due to, 724–25
due to the fact that, 725

each, 725
"Eclipse," 265
editing, 667–744
"Education," 74
effect/affect, 719
e.g./i.e., 725
"Einstein of Happiness, The," 399
either . . . or, 631
"Elapsed Expectations," 184
elegant variation, 481
ellipsis, 675
emphasis, 490–501
empty conclusions, 440
empty words, 435–44
encyclopedias, 317
    bibliographic reference to, 352
enthuse, 725
Ephron, Nora
    "A Few Words about Breasts:
    Shaping Up Absurd," 599
essay examinations, 411–18
et cetera/et alii, 725–26
"Ethnobotanists Race Against
    Time," 403

euphemisms, 468
euphony, 482
Evans, Bergen
    "Sophistication," 131
everybody/everyone, 726
evidence
    presenting, 188–89
    suppressing, 196–97
examinations, 411–18
examples/instances, 729
examples, use of, 458–60
except/accept, 719
exclamation mark, 490
exists, 726
explication, 389–91
exposition, 154–69
expound/explain, 726
extra clauses, 444–47
extra words, 435–44

facet, 726
factor, 726
fact that, the, 726
fallacies, 195–200
false comparison, 731
false series, 474
famous/notorious, 726
"Farm Picture, A," 244
farther/further, 727
fatalistic/pessimistic, 727
"Fathers and Sons," 644
"Few Words about Breasts, A:
    Shaping Up Absurd," 599
fewer/less, 730
field of, 721
Finch, Robert
    "Very Like a Whale," 607
first/firstly, 727
first person, use of, 471–72
"Fish Eat Brazilian Fisherman,"
    103
"Flag, The," 555

"Flea, The," 210
fluency, 540–51
focus, 13–14, 26
footnotes, 342–43
formal outline, 79–80
formal writing, 510–13
former/latter, 727
Forster, E. M.
"My Wood," 525
found poems, 537–38
"Four Letter Words Can Hurt You," 213
fragment, sentence, 497–98, 680–82
Franklin, Benjamin, 531–32
Freeman, Patricia
"The Einstein of Happiness," 399
"friends that have it I do wrong, The," 427
further/farther, 727

Garred, Eileen
"Ethnobotanists Race Against Time," 403
"Gaucho and the City, The: Stories of Horsemen," 588
general, 18–20
generalization, 197
genetic fallacy, 197–98
"Glenn Stribling," 644
Glossary of Usage, 719–41
good/well, 727
Goodman, Paul
"A Proposal to Abolish Grading," 613
graduate/graduate from, 727
graduate programs, applications for, 425–26
"Graduation," 286
"Grant and Lee: A Study in Contrasts," 70

Greenfield, Jeff
"Columbo Knows the Butler Didn't Do It," 64
Groucho Marx complex, 24

he or she/his or her, 727
"High Horse's Courting," 297
his or her/he or she, 727
"Hitch Haiku," 500
hopefully/I hope, 728
"How Cemeteries Bring Us Back to Earth," 250
"How to Get Things Done," 572
however, 690, 728
"How to Deal with the Crying," 159
"How to Grow an Avocado," 160
hyphen, 700–02

"I," 471–72
idea that, the, 728
identify, 728
idioms, 718
i.e./e.g., 728
I hope/hopefully, 728
"Iks, The," 522
illusion/allusion, 720
imitation, 531–32, 534–35
immanent/imminent, 729
imply/infer, 729
"Indecent Exposure," 172
independent clause, 497
individual, 729
induction, 197, 202
infer/imply, 729
infinitive, 736
informal writing, 510–15
"In Search of the Elusive Pingo," 155
instances/examples, 729
instant prose, 432–35

intensifiers, weak, 437
interviews, 398–411
introductory clauses, 689
introductory paragraphs, 105–09
invention, 7–13, 41
irony, 12, 194, 735
irregardless/regardless, 729
italics, 698–99
it is, 446–47, 729
its/it's, 729
"It's the Portly Penguin That Gets
    the Girl, French Biologist
    Claims," 175

Jacobs, Jane
    "The Use of Sidewalks," 255
Jacoby, Susan
    "Too Many Women Are
      Misconstruing Feminism's
      Nature," 233
Janeway, Elizabeth
    "Soaps, Cynicism, and Mind
      Control," 616
jargon, 462–64
"Jimmy Buffett Is Going
    Coconuts?!" 396
jobs, letters for, 421–25
"Joey: A 'Mechanical Boy,'" 577
journal, 540–51
"Journals of Sylvia Plath," 544

Kael, Pauline, 514
Kennedy, X. J., "Who Killed
    King Kong?" 620
kind of, 729
King, Martin Luther
    "Nonviolent Resistance," 67
Klein, Carole
    "The Tough Got Going," 393
Koch, Edward I.
    "Death and Justice: How

    Capital Punishment Affirms
    Life," 237
Kozol, Jonathan
    "Operation Illiteracy," 231
Kraemer, Chuck
    "Indecent Exposure," 172

latter/former, 727
Lawrence, Barbara
    "Four Letter Words Can Hurt
    You," 213
lay/lie, 729
lend/loan, 730
less/fewer, 730
"Lesson, A," 20
letter (on rape), 273
letters, covering, 421–25
levels of usage, 510–15
Lewis, C. S.
    "The Trouble with 'X'. . .,"
    624
library card, 312–15
lie/lay, 729
Lightman, Alan P.
    "Elapsed Expectations," 184
lifestyle/life-style/life style, 730
like/as, 721
literally, 730
literature, examinations in, 413–15
loan/lend, 730
logic, 189, 195–203
loose/lose,7306
"Los Angeles Notebook," 262
"Love Is a Fallacy," 218
"Love Poem," 485

main clause, 497
majority, 730
Malcolm X
    "Rejected," 283
"Male Myth, The," 150
man/mankind, 730

Mandelbaum, Anne Hebald
 "It's the Portly Penguin That
  Gets the Girl, French Biologist Claims," 175
manuscript form, 669–72
margins, 670
Margolis, Jack
 "And All Those Others," 537
Martin, Lynda
 "Adman's Atlanta," 259
mathematics, examinations in,
  416–18
may/can, 723
me, 730

Mead, Margaret
 "On Friendship," 134
"Mechanic's Feel," 130
media/medium, 730–31
metaphor
 mixed, 465–67
 use of, 465–67
Metraux, Rhoda
 "On Friendship," 134
Miller, Jonathan
 "The Body in Question," 177
misplaced modifiers, 475–76
misquotation, 196
mixed metaphors, 465–67
MLA format, 333–54
modifiers
 dangling, 476–77
 misplaced, 475–76
 nonrestrictive, 691–92
 restrictive, 691–92
 squinting, 476–77
more, 731
most/almost, 731
"My Wood," 525

narration, 248–50, 267–75
nature of, the, 731

needless to say, 731
negative constructions, 443–44
Negro, 731
neither . . . nor, 725
Nemerov, Howard, 513
"Newark Public Library, The," 8
"News Item," 691
"New Science Center at Wellesley
  College—an Eyesore?" 216
"New Solution for the C.I.A.,
  A," 228
"Nitrites: Cancer for Many,
  Money for Few," 357
Nixon, Richard, 537
nobody/no one/none, 731
nonrestrictive modifier, 691–92
"Nonviolent Resistance," 67
notes, taking, 323–25
not only . . . but also, 731
not . . . un-, 731
notorious/famous, 726
number/amount, 720
number of, a, 732
numbers, 704–06

obscurity, 450–53
O'Connor, Flannery
 "Total Effect and the Eighth
  Grade," 628
of/have, 732
off of/off, 732
often-times, 732
old-fashioned/old-fashion, 732
"On Friendship," 134
one/he, 732
one of, 732
"On Keeping a Notebook," 592
only, 476, 733
"On Natural Death," 652
"Operation Illiteracy," 231
oral/verbal, 739

organization
of arguments, 203–04
of book reviews, 392
of comparisons, 50–52
of descriptions, 244–45
of essays on a process, 159–63
of expository essays, 162–63
of narration, 271
of paragraphs, 90–93
of persuasive essays, 203–04
of research papers, 329–32
Orwell, George
"Politics and the English
Language," 631
"Shooting an Elephant," 276
other, 733
outline, 42, 77–81, 358–59

pagination of manuscript, 670
paragraphs, 82–117
concluding, 109–13
introductory, 105–09
length of, 101–05
organization of, 90–93
outline, 78–79
symbol for, 672
transitions between, 98–99
transitions in, 95–96
parallel construction, 483–86
paraphrase, 326–27, 532–34
parentheses, 695–96
Parker, Dorothy
"News Item," 691
Parsons, Talcott, 513
particular, 18–20
passive voice, 469–71
per, 733
per cent, percent, percentage, 733–
34
period, 684–85

periodicals, indexes to, 318–20
Perrin, Noel
"The Androgynous Man," 146
per se, 734
persona, 194–95, 506
persuasion, 188–204
pessimistic/fatalistic, 727
phenomena/phenomenon, 734
physical sciences, examinations in,
416–18
Pillow Book of Sei Shōnagon, The,
546
Pirsig, Robert M.
"Mechanic's Feel," 130
plagiarism, 326–29
Plath, Sylvia
"Journals," 544
plays, citations of, 340, 706
plurals, unusual, 703
plus, 734
point of view, 246–48
politics, 734
"Politics and the English
Language," 631
Pope, Susan
"Tennis Tips to a Beginning
Player," 156
possessive, 702–03
post hoc ergo propter hoc, 199
predicate(s), 496–97
prejudice/prejudiced, 734
premises, 201–03
preventative/preventive, 734
primary material, 310
prior to, 734
process, 159–62
professional programs,
applications for, 425–26
"Professions for Women," 515
pronouns
possessive, 702

reference of, 477–79
shift in, 478
proofreading, 671
"Proposal to Abolish Grading,
A," 613
protagonist, 734
punctuation, 678–710
"Putting the Outside Inside the
Fence of Law," 211

qualifiers, weak, 437, 492
questions, asking and answering,
7–13, 15, 26–27, 41
quite, 437, 734
quotation/quote, 734
quotation marks, 672–77, 696–98
as apologies, 456–57, 697
with other punctuation, 334,
698
with titles, 676, 697
single, 676, 696
quotations, form of, 330–31, 334
edited, 674–75
embedded, 333–35, 674–75
set off, 335, 341, 673–74

rather, 437, 734–35
"Reach of Imagination, The," 138
reader, 15–18, 28
reading and taking notes, 322–25
reasoning, 189–90, 195–200
reason . . . is because, the, 735
rebut/refute, 735
redundancy, 442–43
reference books, 320–21
reference of pronouns, 477–79
refute/rebut, 735
regardless, irregardless, 729
regard to, 735
"Rejected," 283
relate to, 735
repel/repulse, 735

repetition, 97–98, 442–43
emphasis by, 495–96
and variation, 481–82
research paper, 309–86
restrictive modifier, 691–92
résumés, 418–21
reviews, writing, 391–98
revising, 28, 429–501
revisions in manuscript, 670–72
Roth, Philip
"The Newark Public Library," 8
run-on sentence, 682–84

Sakamoto, Nancy
"Conversational Ballgames,"
180
sarcasm, 194, 697, 735
satire, 506
scene vs. summary, 270–71
"Science of Deduction, The," 52
scratch outline, 42, 77–78
secondary material, 310
second/secondly, 727
seem, 735
Sei Shōnagon
The Pillow Book of Sei Shōnagon,
546
self, writing about, 20–25
semiannually/biannually, 723
semicolon, 686–88
semimonthly/bimonthly, 723
semiweekly/biweekly, 723
sentence(s)
cumulative, 534–36
defined, 496–97
extra, 444–46
fragment, 497–98
kinds of, 496–98
run-on, 682–84
short and long, 492–95
structure, 483–86

series, true and false, 474
sexism in language (see *he or she*
    and *man/mankind,* 727, 730)
shall/will, 736
"Shooting an Elephant," 276
should/would, 736
Shulman, Max
    "Love Is a Fallacy," 218
simple sentence, 496–97
simplistic/simplify, 736
since/because, 736
situation, 736
Snyder, Gary
    "Hitch Haiku," 500
"Soaps, Cynicism, and Mind
    Control," 616
social sciences, examinations in,
    415–16
"Sophistication," 131
sorting, 37–43
sources, acknowledging, 326–29
specific, 18–20, 457–58
spelling, 711–16
split infinitives, 736
squinting modifiers, 476–77
stanza/verse, 739
stipulative definition, 123–24
Stone, Christopher D.
    "Putting the Outside Inside the
        Fence of Law," 211
Stone, I. F.
    "A New Solution for the
        C.I.A.," 228
"Stranger in the Village," 560
Strehlow, Rebecca W.
    "The New Science Center at
        Wellesley College—An
        Eyesore?" 216
style, 505–39
subject, 13, 311
    of a sentence, 496–97
    versus topic, 13

subjunctive, 736–37
subordinate clause, 497
subordinating conjunction, 681–
    82, 683
subordination, 444–47, 496–500
    emphasis, 497–500
summary, 44, 163–69, 323–24, 532
    in narrative, 270–71
syllabification, 701–02
syllogism, 202
"Symbolism," 537–38
synthesis, 48

teacher, writer as, 15–18
technical language, 462–64
Temple, Lisa
    "Beyond the Institution: The
        Effects of Labeling on Ex-
        Mental Patients," 373
"Tennis Tips to a Beginning
    Player," 156
Terkel, Studs
    "Fathers and Sons," 644
texture, 529–30
than/then, 737
that, 445–46
that/which/who, 737
their/there/they're, 737
then/than, 737
there is, there are, 446–47
Theroux, Paul
    "The Male Myth," 150
thesis, 13–15, 26–27, 311–12
this, 737
this is, 446–47
Thomas, Lewis
    "On Natural Death," 652
    "The Iks," 522
Thoreau, Henry David
    "The Battle of the Ants," 654
Thurow, Lester

"Why Women Are Paid Less Than Men," 658
thus/thusly, 738
till/until, 738
title(s)
  capitalization of, 699
  choosing a, 27
  form at head of manuscript, 670
  italicization of, 344–45, 684–85, 698
  of parts of the Bible, 677
  use of quotation marks with, 684, 697
title page, 357, 670
to, too, two, 738
to be, problems with the verb, 440–41
to have, problems with the verb, 441–42
"To Lie or Not to Lie? — The Doctor's Dilemma," 586
to make, problems with the verb, 441–42
tone, 507–15
too, 738
"Too Many Women Are Misconstruing Feminism's Nature," 233
topic, 13–15, 311
topic ideas, 85, 87
topic of/area of, 721
topic sentences, 84–86
"Total Effect and the Eighth Grade," 628
"Tough Got Going, The," 393
toward/towards, 738
transformations, 536–37
transitions, 94–99, 483
"Trouble with 'X' . . ., The," 624
two, 738
type/type of, 738

typographical errors, revision of, 670–71

underlining, 698
uninterested/disinterested, 724
unique, 437, 738
unity (in paragraphs), 82, 84–90
until/till, 738
Updike, John
  "Beer Can," 521
U.S./United States, 738
usage, 717–41
  levels of, 510–15
usage/use, 738
use of, 738
"Use of Sidewalks, The," 255
utilize/utilization, 738

variation, 481–82
variety, in sentences, 492–95, 496–500
verbal/oral, 739
verse/stanza, 739
very, 437
"Very Like a Whale," 607
viable, 739
voice, active and passive, 469–71

was, were, 739
we, 739
well/good, 727
well-known/widely known, 739
were, was, 739
which, 445–46, 739
which/that/who, 737
while, 739
White, E. B.
  "The Door," 661
  "Education," 74
Whitehead, Alfred North, 514
Whitman, Walt
  "A Farm Picture," 244

who, 445–46, 740
who/that/which, 737
who/whom/whomever, 740
"Who Killed King Kong?" 620
whoever/whomever, 740
who's/whose, 740
"Why Women Are Paid Less Than Men," 658
widely known/well-known, 739
will/shall, 736
wit, 191–94
with regard to, 735
Woolf, Virginia
    "Professions for Women," 515
word processing, 4, 29–32, 330, 385, 716

wordiness, 431–49
works cited, list of, 343–54
would, 740
would/should, 736
writer as teacher, 15–18

Yeats, William Butler
    "The Balloon of the Mind," 1, 389
    "The friends that have it I do wrong," 427
you, 740–41
your/you're, 741

Zen anecdote, 503
zonkers, 432–34